IMPACT ALONG THE EDGE

A NATURAL HISTORY OF
SHALLENBERGER STATE NATURE PRESERVE

IMPACT ALONG THE EDGE

JIM OSBORN

proving
press

BOOK DESIGN & PRODUCTION:
COLUMBUS PUBLISHING LAB
WWW.COLUMBUSPUBLISHINGLAB.COM

PAPERBACK ISBN: 978-1-63337-801-8
E-BOOK ISBN: 978-1-63337-802-5

PRINTED IN THE UNITED STATES OF AMERICA
1 3 5 7 9 10 8 6 4 2

COVER PHOTOGRAPHS: VIEW TOWARD THE NORTHWEST
FROM THE TOP OF ALLEN KNOB (TOP) AND
TRILLIUM BLOOM IN SPRING (BOTTOM).

TABLE OF CONTENTS

Hepatica in peak bloom on March 29, 2017. The narrow, leafy plants coming up around the hepatica are cut-leaved toothworts. Both species indicate a stable forest environment, a protected remnant of our natural history.

PREFACE

AFTER DEFEATING the Native Americans at Fallen Timbers, Anglo-European settlers started flowing into Ohio. Revolutionary War veterans, immigrants, speculators, and farmers raced for the new lands just released for sale; in just eight short years Ohio petitioned for statehood. The twin sandstone knobs, Allen and Ruble, at Shallenberger State Nature Preserve would never be the same.

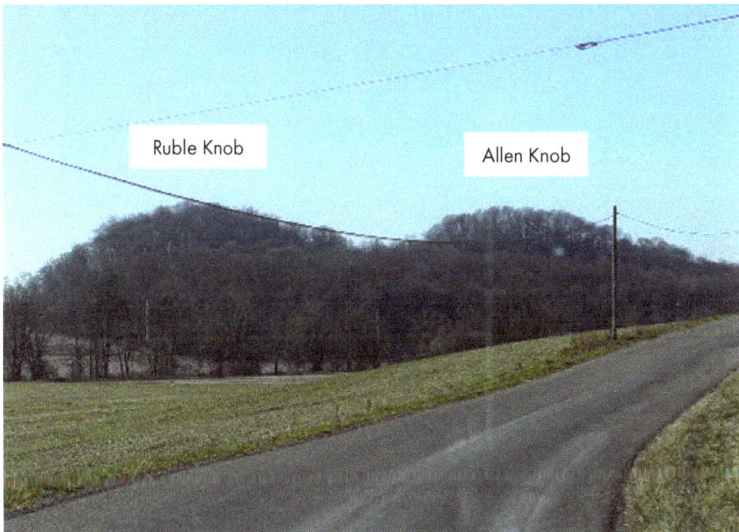

Traveling west on Crumley Road. Looking at the northeast side of Ruble and Allen Knob.

The explosion of tourism and urbanism in the Hocking Hills Region of southeast Ohio brings a modern diaspora. Tourists and commuters heading south on US Route 33 to live or play in the hills pass by the sandstone knobs that herald a shift from the flat, gently rolling land of the north and west into the hill country of the south and east.

The conical Beck's Knob is directly north of the twin knobs. Slightly to its northeast is Claypool Knob. Mount Pleasant, a sandstone block that rises above Lancaster, is visible even farther to the northeast. A long, shallow ridgeline runs to the northwest, containing the Franklin County Metro Parks' Chestnut Ridge. David Rains Wallace made the landmark famous with his 1980 work *Idle Weeds: The Life of an Ohio Sandstone Ridge*.

Wallace writes of Chestnut Ridge, "Of course, it made no difference to the ridge whether civilization used it as a park or housing development for one or two ticks of its geological clock's second hand. But this benign neglect offered an opportunity to observe the ridge as one that might watch a wild animal that has been kept captive and allowed to run loose again."

This story adds another 40 years to the "clock" from 1980 to the present day at Shallenberger, a clock that began literally buried in the deep history of ancient seas and mountains long gone. Immense geological forces and glaciation resulted in the creation of the twin knobs, Allen and Ruble. In the "one or two clicks" since the Anglo-European settlers arrived, Shallenberger has felt the full force of sudden change. After sweeping Native Americans aside, European settlers and global commerce combined to change the course of natural history, impacting the animals and plants that formed the rich carpet of life that had spread

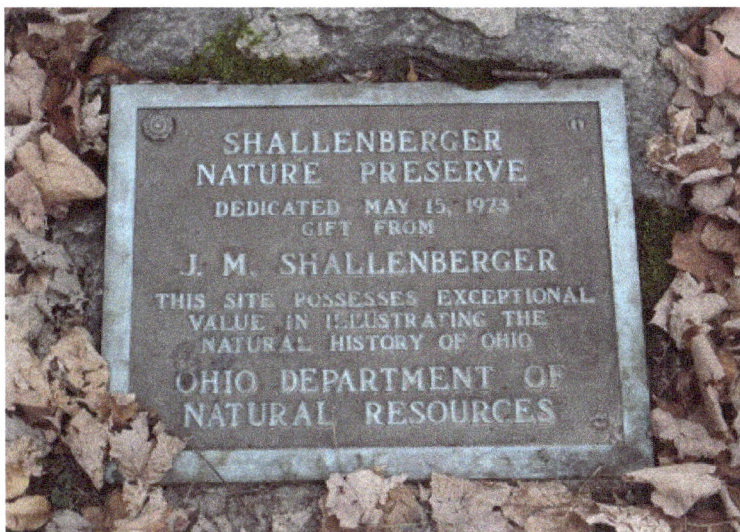

Dedication plaque on the right side of the trail at the entrance.

Trillium blooming on the north west slope of Allen Knob. April 23, 2015.

both ways across the divide. The original mix of plant and animal species quickly transformed into new combinations of original and exotic species, while humans shattered the sandstone crowns with drills and black powder.

Meteorites, volcanism, and climate change have also shifted the makeup of creation repeatedly over time spans stretching beyond human comprehension. The frightening aspect of the change at Shallenberger is that it has occurred within a few human generations and, in some cases, within a single human lifespan.

A farsighted man saw the injured knobs and put an end to the madness of exploitation and destruction. Jay Shallenberger must have loved these two knobs and named the scarred twins after his own children, Allen and Ruble. He transferred the 88 acres of land containing Allen and Ruble to the Fairfield County Commissioners in 1971. In turn, Fairfield County transferred the property to the Ohio Department of Natural Resources' Department of Natural Areas and Preserves (DNAP) and was dedicated as a state nature preserve on May 15, 1973. Throughout the modern story of Shallenberger's history, DNAP, with its paid and volunteer personnel, looms large in the preservation and restoration of the site. The creation of Shallenberger State Nature Preserve designated a part of this topographical edge as protected land, allowing "a wild animal to run loose again."

INTRODUCTION TO SHALLENBERGER

THE DRIVE SOUTHEAST out of Columbus toward Lancaster on US Route 33 is flat to gently rolling. Near the Carroll exit, 10 miles north of Lancaster, the road splits. Business Route 33 shepherds traffic into Lancaster while a limited-access freeway speeds travelers to the west toward Shallenberger.

Upon approaching the exit for Route 188, the topography begins to change. Conical shaped rocky knobs rise suddenly out

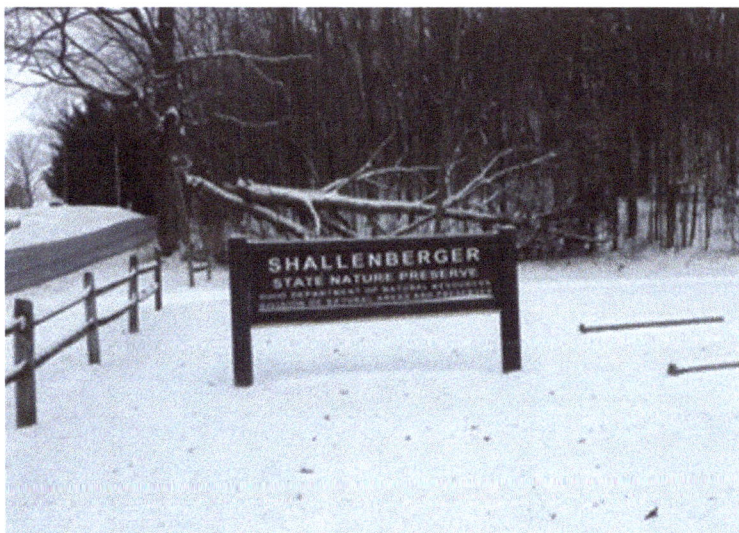

Find the preserve at: 2468 Becks Knob Road SW, Lancaster, Ohio 43130.

*View from Allen Knob to the North, Beck's Knob is on the right.
Notice the flatter land beyond Beck's Knob.*

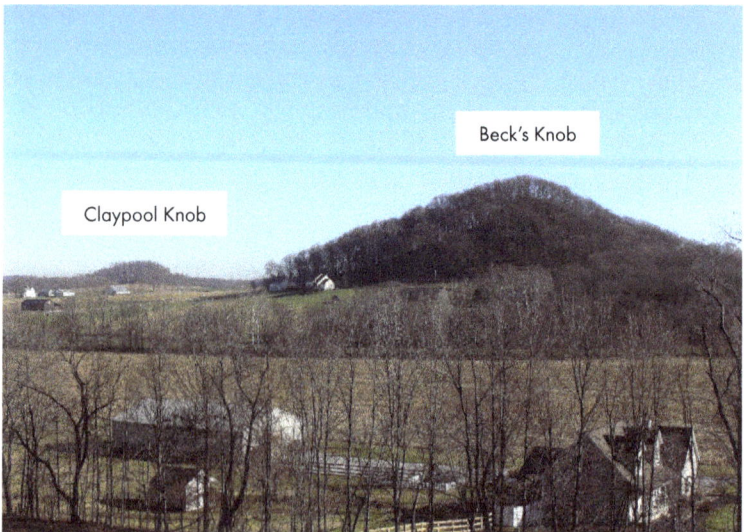

*Shallenberger is to the right in this photo, illustrating two other sandstone knobs
southeast of Lancaster. Allen and Ruble Knob are just out of sight to the left.*

of flat fields on the left with ridgelines rising above the highway on the right. The highway rises gently toward the exit for State Route 22 while passing the twin knobs at Shallenberger on the north. Almost immediately after turning toward Lancaster on Route 22, the turn lane onto Becks Knob Road appears on the left. After turning onto Becks Knob Road, the knobs fill the windshield, and within a quarter-mile, the Shallenberger State Nature Preserve sign and parking lot become visible.

The aerial view of Shallenberger below illustrates its position, sandwiched in between the State Route 33 bypass and State Route 22 with its western edge bordered by Becks Knob Road.

Farmers' fields and homes line the edges of the preserve while Hunter's Run, a small stream, defines its northern boundary. The yellow line on the map represents the preserve's trail system, and

Trail system at Shallenberger in yellow. Map courtesy of Ohio Department of Natural Areas and Preserves. North is up.

the cone-like contour lines designate the knobs: Allen to the west, and Ruble to the east. The preserve boundary is outlined in black.

Shallenberger Nature Preserve contains almost two miles of trails, featuring a spur trail near the top of Allen Knob that leads to the overlook pictured on page two. The trail meanders in a figure eight-fashion, circling around Allen Knob with a connector to the east side linking to another loop that circles below the north slope of Ruble Knob.

The story in this book goes beyond the rock that formed the knobs; the covering of the trees, shrubs, and forbs are discussed along with human impact and introduction of non-native species. While wandering along the trails, a careful observer can peer back into the natural history of Ohio. It is a sincere hope that an appreciation of change, both long- and short-term, influences our thinking of how we take care of our few remaining wild places.

BEGINNINGS

TAKE THE SPUR TRAIL toward Allen Knob and climb up the staircase. Stop for a minute and spend some time with the rock. The hardened blocks of sandstone were the crumbs of ancient mountains. The honeycomb-like pits hint at the number of years through which this rock was exposed to the elements and the way in which it was cemented together.

Long ago, there was an era of colliding continents, each riding its own tectonic plate, all mashing into each other. As fast as the mountains were thrust up along the edges, they were eroded down again. During this time, Ohio was the bottom of a shallow sea to the west of the conflict zone.

You might see little, white pebbles embedded in the sand of the path. Freezing and thawing finally caused a quartz rock to break free, and it sped off the mountainside with the force of a hard rain. Caught in a raging current with no way to escape, the rock went careening down the miles of canyons while banging, rubbing, and splintering alongside other, similar rocks. The fractured angles broke off, and over time and distance, the rock was ground into pebbles and sand.

One of the pebbles, like the rest, was gradually worn smooth by its travels. The water slowed, allowing it to settle down and drift alongside the sand with which it traveled, trapped in the current of an ancient river. More sand and pebbles settled on top of it. The finer silts and clays pushed farther beyond this point before settling in the ocean. The milky white pebble came to rest in a sandy grave and remembers the once-beautiful majesty of the mountains before they vanished into the fog of the far past.

Born from the crumbs of ancient mountains, hardened by the sea, pushed up into the light, riding an arch up and out of the waves, came two siblings, Allen and Ruble.

Fresh and youthful, they stood on the edge of a great plateau, guarding the dark hills behind them.

Locally known as "party rock," this sandstone boulder greets hikers near the first trail split. At some point, this boulder separated en masse from Allen Knob above and came to rest here. Look at it lying there, partially buried, and wonder, "How did that happen?"

As is true of rocks found everywhere in Ohio, Allen and Ruble were born of rock participating in the perennial game of the rock cycle. According to this cycle, larger rock weathers upon exposure to sun, cold, rain, and wind. Erosion begins, and sediments blow or flow around until they pile up and get pressed and glued back into rock again.[1] In comparison to this process, the human timeline moves from conception through the periods of childhood and adulthood towards death in a short linear sequence. The birth and existence of Allen and Ruble have followed a similarly linear path but extend through ages, both past and future, that human eyes did not or will not ever view.

The ebb and flow of various iterations of the rock cycle has produced different vistas across Ohio. The evidence of this cycle, different types of bedrock, lies covered by glacial till in the west and peeks out through the thin soils of the hills in the south and east. The Ohio Department of Natural Resources' Division of Geological Survey helps to explain the rock's deep past by using maps that illustrate the bedrock and other glacial impacts that have occurred across the state.

The story of Shallenberger started around 360 million years ago, when Ohio was part of a shallow basin in a larger ocean. Mountains to the east dumped eroded sandstone, shales, and pieces of quartz into this basin,[2] slowly moving the shoreline west over deeper water. Iron oxides, along with silicates,[3] dissolved in the seawater and interacted with the finer sands and small pebbles,

1 The word "deposition" is often used to refer to eroded materials piling up someplace while on their journey to become rock.

2 Think no further than the washbasin in the bathroom: a low place where water collects, along with sediments that have traveled with it.

3 Silicates: the stuff that makes up most rock, a combination of oxygen and silicon.

tightly cementing the parts together. Over a period of geologic time, the weight of the water and other materials deposited on top of this layer of sand and pebbles began to form part of the bedrock[4] of Fairfield County.

Refer to the map below and look for the dark blue strip of Mississippian Rock. A traveler in the present day, heading south near the US 33 Lancaster Bypass, will see this bedrock in the road cuts past the exit to Shallenberger. It is within this greater bedrock formation that an erosion-resistant rock initially formed. Due to the discovery of a Native American hand symbol on an outcrop of the rock near Newark, Ohio, it was named Black Hand Sandstone.

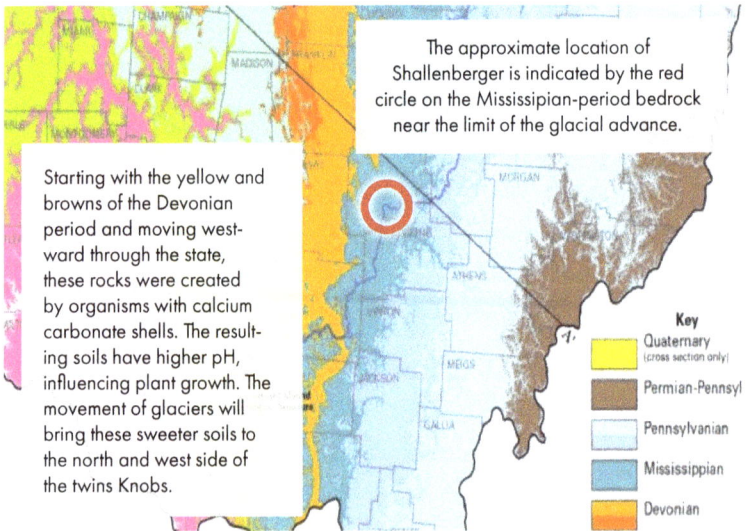

The approximate location of Shallenberger is indicated by the red circle on the Mississipian-period bedrock near the limit of the glacial advance.

Starting with the yellow and browns of the Devonian period and moving westward through the state, these rocks were created by organisms with calcium carbonate shells. The resulting soils have higher pH, influencing plant growth. The movement of glaciers will bring these sweeter soils to the north and west side of the twins Knobs.

Key
Quaternary (cross section only)
Permian-Pennsyl
Pennsylvanian
Mississippian
Devonian

Ohio Division of Geological Survey, 2006. Bedrock Geology Map of Ohio: Ohio Department of Natural Resources, Division of Geological Survey Map BG-1, generalized page size with text 2p., scale 1:200,000.

4 Bedrock: the first layer of solid rock underneath the soil.

Using the analogy of a jawbreaker, the deposition and formation of the Black Hand Sandstone occurred similarly to the way one places a piece of hard candy inside his gum. The Black Hand Sandstone lay buried in the larger Cuyahoga geological formation, almost as if in a tomb, until erosion exposed it. The softer rocks encasing it eventually eroded into rounded hills. The Black Hand Sandstone refused to follow the pattern and formed erosion-resistant cliffs that would later resist the push of ice from the glaciers.

The Black Hand Sandstone extends north from the Hocking Hills through eastern Ohio and dips down to the east at a slight angle. Geologist Karl Var Steeg (1947) reckoned that this rock ranges from "Vinton County in the south into Richland and Ashland Counties to the north, a distance of more than 100 miles." Visitors to Chestnut Ridge Metro Park, Mount Pleasant, Christmas Rocks State Nature Preserve, and Shallenberger can see the western boundaries of this rock. Farther east, it lies under the ridgetops and forms the hollows and gorges of Hocking Hills State Park.

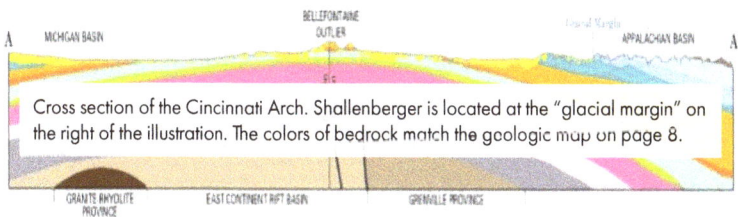

Cross section of the Cincinnati Arch. Shallenberger is located at the "glacial margin" on the right of the illustration. The colors of bedrock match the geologic map on page 8.

This is the bottom portion of the map on page 11. From the Ohio Division of Geological Survey, 2006 Bedrock Geology Map of Ohio: Ohio Department of Natural Resources, Division of Geological Survey Map BG-1, generalized page size with text 2p., scale 1:200,000.

The exposed areas of Black Hand Sandstone near the twin knobs reveal its edge. The bedrock map on page nine illustrates the various layers and suggests that something happened after the deposition of this rock to cut into like a layered cake, exposing the different strata.

This form of honeycomb weathering occurs when water slowly seeps through slightly weaker channels in the fine interior of the sandstone and does what outside forces cannot do: it loosens the glue that binds the grains of sand and pops them out. Notice the dark iron compounds in the sandstone.

The Cincinnati Arch happened: forces within the earth forced a bubble to rise up and enabled Allen and Ruble to ride an arch up and out of the sea. Wolfe, Forsyth and Dove conclude "the single most important event in the preglacial history of Fairfield County, after early Permian time is the regional uplift which brought the Paleozoic strata to their present condition (1960)."[5] Immediately after the uplift, the ever-present forces of erosion went to work on the exposed arch.

5 This is geo babble simply saying the uplift from the Cincinnati Arch literally lay the groundwork (no pun intended) for present day Fairfield County.

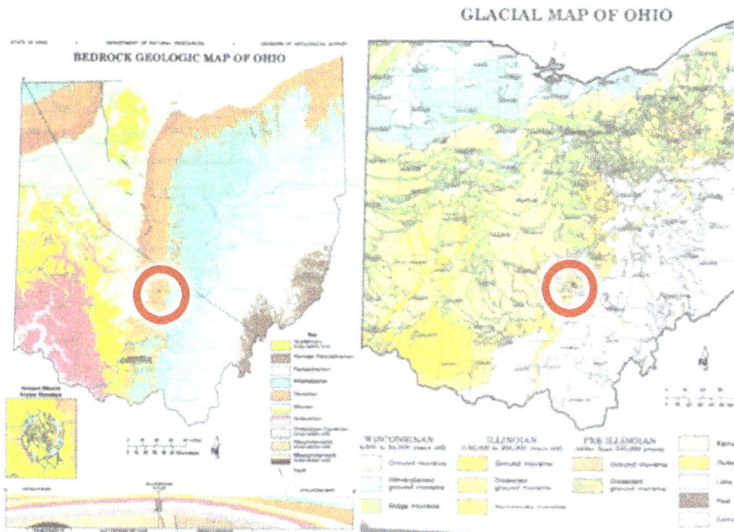

Compare the bedrock map on the left with the map illustrating the extent of glacial flow in Ohio. In both maps, the approximate location of Shallenberger State Nature Preserve is within the red circle. The knobs lie very close to the farthest extent of the glacial ice.

The creation of this arch lifted the bedrock from northern Alabama to Lake Erie. Fairfield County lies on the eastern, rising portion of the uplift. Refer to the Bedrock Geologic Map on the left above and notice its similarities to a layer cake, with the different colors representing rocks of different ages. See where the top of the cake forms a dome in the middle, and imagine slicing it right across the top to make it flat. In the graphic on page 9, erosion did the work of the knife.

Notice how the oldest rock layers in the arch are the limestone-based Silurian Age[6] rocks, which are centered around the Cincinnati area. Columbus sits over Devonian Age rock, while

---

6 The pinkish color on the bedrock map in the southwest corner of the state represents Silurian age bedrock.

*The evidence of glacial activity on the sandstone knobs lies scattered through-
out the north and west sides of Shallenberger. This granite boulder lies near
and is easily visible from the trail on the northwest side of Allen Knob.*

Fairfield County is on the edge of Mississippian Age rocks, containing the embedded Black Hand Sandstone. Pennsylvanian
Age rock lies farther to the east, and the youngest rock in Ohio,
Permian Age rock, is exclusively found in the easternmost parts of
the state. On the uplifted parts of the arch, all the later rock that
was formed during the time in which dinosaurs roamed the earth
was eventually eroded away.

Finally, we have a plausible explanation for why Allen, Ruble,
and nearby Beck's Knob jut so sharply out of otherwise reasonably
gentle terrain. However, there is more to the story of slow-moving
violence along this edge: The sea had been evicted from this part
of Ohio, but it came back as ice.[7]

---

7 Glacial map of Ohio: Ohio Division of Geological Survey, 2006. Glacial Map of Ohio. Ohio

The view looking upslope on the west side of Allen Knob. Notice the glacial erratics embedded along the edge of this old tote road. The wall of ice must have been majestic as it pushed against the knobs.

Earlier glaciations blocked the original river courses, reversing streams and rivers and resulting in the current Scioto and Hocking Rivers. As the ice melted, meltwater created new channels and changed the drainage patterns. Arney Run, which flows east of Shallenberger and through Christmas Rocks State Nature Preserve, along with Clear Creek, which flows through Clear Creek Metro Park and Two Glaciers County Park, are local streams that reversed their courses and cut new channels due to ice blocking their former paths.

According to Richard Goldthwait, an "internationally respected" glacial geologist, Ohio has had more than four separate

Department of Natural Resources, Division of Geological Survey Map, page size with text 2p., scale 1:200,000.

ice ages over the last one million years (Lafferty, 2003). In relation to the knobs, the most significant ice ages are called the Illinoian Age and the Wisconsinan Age. The Illinoian glacier shifted a few miles to the south and east, eventually reaching Christmas Rocks State Nature Preserve. The county glacial map below illustrates the more recent activity of the Wisconsin glacier, which melted down around the knobs.

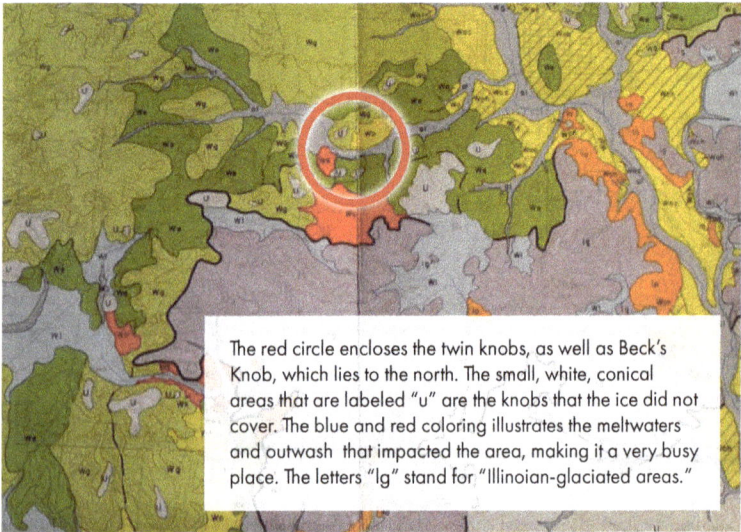

Map from the Geology of Fairfield County (1962). The light green areas are the glacial till resulting from faster-moving ice—think of the gently rolling fields along Route 33 that are visible on the drive south from Columbus. The darker green is end moraine, low ridges where the ice remained stationary, pushing forward while melting back.

Most evidence of early glaciations was destroyed by more recent glaciations. The Illinoian glaciation occurred around 300,000 years ago. It moved a little bit farther to the south and east than the later Wisconsin glaciation. The Wisconsinan glaciation was the most recent, arriving approximately 24,000 years ago and leaving around 14,000 years ago. In central Ohio, the ice sheet may have been up to 1,000 feet thick (Lafferty, 2003).[8]

The green colors on the glacial activity map represent the extent and type of land left behind by the Wisconsin Glacier (ranging from flat to rolling). The extensive red and yellow areas represent distinct types of glacial drift[9] that would later influence Anglo-European settlement: The ice came from the north and west, bringing soil and rock debris from those regions and depositing it as glacial till far from the source. The currents of meltwater that were streaming under and in front of the glaciers mixed soils, leveled the terrain and changed drainage patterns throughout the glaciated area and down major drainages away from the glacial front. The grey color on the map represents eroded remnants of the more ancient Illinoian glaciation.

In summary, the sediments that would ultimately become the twin knobs at Shallenberger hardened into rock. The rock burst upward into the daylight with the Cincinnati Arch, the seas drained away, and the ice arrived. The combined effects of the Cincinnati Arch and glaciation produced the edge that is currently visible from the windshield of a southeast-moving vehicle on US 33. All that is left on this topic is for man to characterize and define the ground forms.

---

8 Actually, the claim in Ohio's Natural History is 1,000 feet at the Fairfield county border. I dispute this, thinking maybe 500 at most due to the absence of glacial erratics on some of the knobs I have been on top of. Reference Lafferty, Michael B., ed. Ohio's Natural Heritage. Columbus: The Ohio Academy of Sciences, 2003. Rich Goldthwait PhD wrote the Chapter "Ice Over Ohio." Erratics are rocks transported from another place by traveling embedded in the ice and left where the ice melts. Ohio sets on sedimentary rock, many of the glacial erratics transported by the ice came from igneous or metamorphic rock in Canada or Michigan.

9 Glacial drift: Sand, soils, and rocks get trapped and scooted along by the ice. As the leading edge of a glacier melts, the heavier stuff settles first out of the meltwater.

The map on page 17, produced by the Ohio Department of Natural Resources' Division of Geological Survey, illustrates the different physiographic regions of Ohio. Physiography is a field of study that analyzes and explains landforms.

Position within the ancient seas, the type of bedrock under the soil, and the presence or absence of glaciers all interacted to craft the different physiographic regions running across Ohio. Bedrock, erosion and glacial activity resulted in different soils forming within different regions. The presence of bedrock materials and glacial till[10] influenced erosion, which shaped the land to provide a surface with various shapes and moisture levels, allowing for numerous species of plant and animals to prosper. Comparing this map with the bedrock and glacial maps of Ohio will reveal some similarities.

The road heading toward Lancaster out of Columbus leaves behind the very flat Columbus Lowland region and passes through the slightly rolling agricultural fields of the Killbuck Glaciated Pittsburgh Plateau. At the point where the road meets the Route 22 exit, ridges rise on the right side of the road while the three sandstone knobs, Beck's, Allen, and Ruble, are visible on the left side. Farm fields shift suddenly to wooded ridges, and by the time the traveler arrives at Sugar Grove, they have passed through the Illinoian Glaciated Allegheny Plateau. Once they reach Logan, they have entered the unglaciated Shawnee-Mississippian Plateau. After the Route 22 exit, the traveler loses sight of the gently

---

10 Glacial till is soil, gravel, sand, and rock mixture left after the glaciers receded. Depending on how fast a glacier melted and what was embedded in the ice, the resulting soils can have different proportions of the parent materials. The flat to gently rolling lands of the Columbus lowlands and the Killbuck Glaciated Plateau, located along Route 33 heading southeast out of Columbus, both contain examples of glacial till. Glacial till starts as dirt, but the action of microbes, fungi, plants, and animals eventually turn that dirt into soil.

undulating farm fields and begins to notice steep-sided timbered hills. This is the edge of which Shallenberger State Nature Preserve protects a small part.

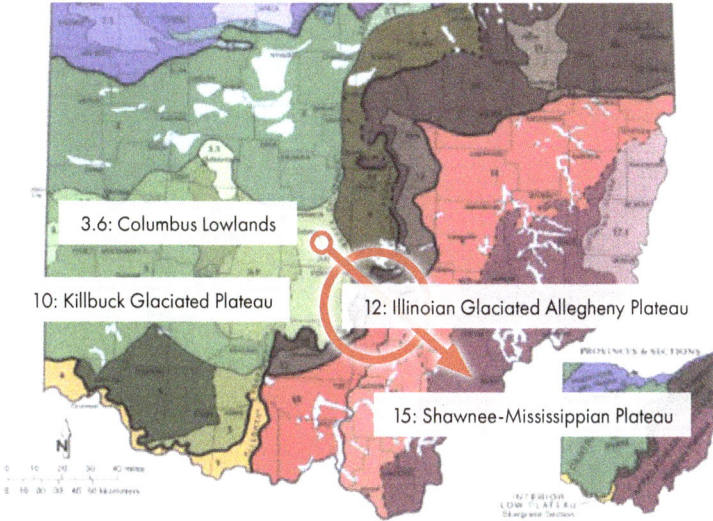

3.6: Columbus Lowlands

10: Killbuck Glaciated Plateau

12: Illinoian Glaciated Allegheny Plateau

15: Shawnee-Mississippian Plateau

Ohio Division of Geological Survey, 1998, Physiographic Regions of Ohio: Ohio Department of Natural Resources, Division of Geological Survey, page size map with text, 2 p., scale 1:2,100,000. The red arrow approximates the direction of US 33 southeast out of Columbus.

The photo on page eighteen is an aerial photograph from the Fairfield County Soil Survey, and the overlaid shapes and abbreviations represent soil types within the preserve. Glacial deposits over the underlying bedrock combined to form a system of at least nine different soil types within the preserve. For example, the soils in the northwest, left behind by the Wisconsinan Glacier, carried ground limestone in the rill. In comparison, in the land up against the knobs on the north side, the glacier left a moraine of deep soil and rock mixture that it had carried from elsewhere. These soils became the basis for the rich wildflower populations present in the area. On the knobs themselves, Loudonville and Steinberg soils formed in the thin tills over the sandstone. Some of the till was carried up there by winds: as the ice melted, dust storms picked up soil from the drying, barren ground in the plains to the west and north before vegetation could get a foothold.

The various types of soil play an important role in the wildlife that populates the area. The outcrop of acidic sandstone that resisted the glacier provides the base for the acid-loving mountain laurel, blueberries, and chestnut oaks that form a ring around Allen Knob and occupy the top of Ruble Knob. The deep glacial deposits on the slopes of the knobs provide support for the special wildflowers that call Shallenberger home.

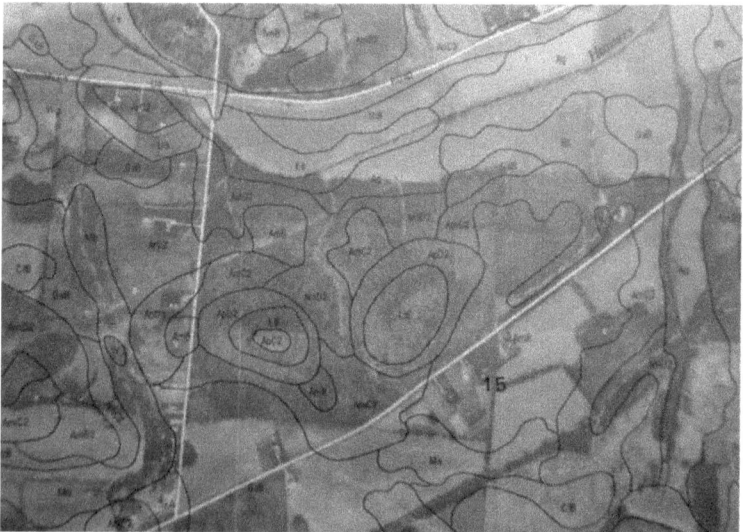

US Department of Agriculture Natural Resources Service, Fairfield County, Ohio. Lancaster NW Quadrangle Sheet Number 28 of 51.

The uplifted Appalachian plateau absorbed the impact from glaciers moving out of the north and west, leaving noticeable wrinkles and knobs where flat to gently rolling land morphed into steep-sided hills. The stage was set for life to explode across the twin knobs. Australian scientist Tim Flannery (2001)[11], when commenting on the tilth of soils and the fate of the peoples and their economies in a given region, asked, "Did you have a good ice age?" Ohio had good ice ages and possessed deep tills that became fertile soils. The edge is formed, and it survived the impact of ice.

Far to the east, beyond the ocean, another type of impact was growing in power and technology. In the distant future, white-sailed ships would bring hammer blows to the twins that rivaled the glaciers.

---

11 Flannery, Tim. 2001. *The Eternal Frontier*. New York: Atlantic Monthly.

ANGLO-EUROPEAN IMPACT ON THE KNOBS

IN *CAPITALISM* *in America: A History* by Alan Greenspan and Adrian Wooldridge, the authors discuss a concept called "creative destruction." How can a term from a book on economics be relevant to a book on natural history? This term implies that something must go away so another thing can replace it. To do so requires an impact of some type. As in economics and warfare, the natural world has proven it participates in "creative

Stone Wall Cemetery, located at 2375 Stonewall Cemetery Road SW in Lancaster, Ohio. In order to completely understand Impact Along the Edge, this is a must-see site. Photo courtesy of Judd Clover.

destruction" through long dead plants and animals frozen in the rock of the past.

To grasp the term "creative destruction," think about how the canal system became defunct once the railroads arrived. This must have been a bummer, especially for the Irish workers who dedicated so much time and effort to digging them. Later, the car and the tractor came along, and horses found themselves unemployed and headed for the glue factory. Similarly, when a big chain such as Walmart shows up on the edge of town, downtown shopping suddenly gets lonely. When rifles arrived on the frontier, bows lost their impact.

Tectonic plates move continents, and oceans come and go with the ebbing and swelling of land masses. Magma is extruded, cools, and erodes into sediments that are carried out to sea and buried under a subduction plate before becoming magma again. Mountains are thrust up and then erode, sending their sediment into rivers that carry them back to the sea in little pieces.

Erosion and deposition continually change the faces of the continents. Warmth comes and goes. Flows of ice bulldoze the whole thing, and it starts over again. The mighty T. rex lies buried in Wyoming, while mammoths tread the cold ground beneath the knobs. Since the time of these ancient creatures, humans arrived from Asia, the climate warmed, the ice retreated, and the mammoth began his trek to the fossil record. New dynamics between plants and animals formed, while fire, flint, and rock tools enabled a successful human entrance into North America.

The tundra around the knobs followed the ice in its retreat north, dragging the fir and spruce trees behind them. The oaks and maples crept north out of their refuges in the south, setting the stage for a new play. Throughout time, the land constantly changes and creates new tapestries for life that must either change with the land or perish.

This story can only speculate on the impact early arriving humans had on the plains and hills that lie within view of the twins. Without fear, large ice age mammals faced the newcomers, perhaps to their complete demise. Flores (2022) asks who or what caused the extinction of these large animals. This may be answered by a combination of climate change and the Stone Age technology wielded by the newly arriving humans. Maybe Allen and Ruble thought nothing of the arrival: what would a flint clovis point do to the sandstone sides that granite boulders could not?

The mound building civilizations of the Adena and the Hopewell probably knew of the twin knobs. In his writings, Graham (1883) reports finding at least 20 different Native American earthworks across the county. After the collapse of the mound builders, time passed quietly until the arrival of Europeans on the continent.

Eastern Native American tribes that traded with the Dutch, English, and French gained access to firearms. The beaver acted as an unwilling catalyst in the conflicts to come as Native American tribes went to war with each other to satisfy the European lust for beaver hats. The twins may have watched in sadness as beavers were exploited in Hunter's Run to their north and Arney Run to their south.

For half a century, most of Ohio remained unoccupied as militant groups in conflict with the Iroquois tribe continually moved both east and west across the future state. Perhaps Allen and Ruble could hear the first booming sounds of gunpowder, something they would later feel. The Europeans, even without direct contact in the Ohio Valley, had already set in motion events that would ultimately weaken the tribes. Eventually, explorers, traders, and settlers would arrive in the area with diseases, steel weapons, steel tools, and domesticated animals that would tip the balance of power in their favor.

A land as rich as Ohio could not stay empty for long. Despite the claims and ferocity of the Iroquois, pressure from European settlements to the east forced the Shawnee, Wyandot, and Delaware tribes to move into Ohio prior to the French and Indian Wars.

European national ambitions over the area collided with this migration, causing wars to erupt between the Europeans and the Native Americans. The prevalence of competitive hunting and trapping decreased beaver populations, resulting in drastic changes to North American waterways. Overhunting drastically lessened bear, elk, and woodland bison populations.

With the beaver population greatly diminished, the next prize for the conflicting groups to fight over was land. Native American and European land philosophies differed relating to the issue of land ownership: Native Americans never thought of themselves as owners of the land. They could seamlessly move between different villages upon need, and hunting parties did not fret over posting "Do Not Trespass" signs, except where there were tribal hostilities. Unsurprisingly, these hostilities ramped up as European nations started wars over North American territory and the tribes were forced to align with either France or England as their dependence on European goods increased.

"It would take nearly two centuries between the first European contact with the Ohio Country and the close of the frontier soon after the war of 1812." Hurt (1996)

It was probably quiet around the twins; maybe they did not witness the fighting. Behind the knobs lay the hill country with its sharp ravines, while in front of them were the till plains. The Wyandot people found the glacial edge along the Hocking River appealing: with fertile land for farming and the combination of hill country, plains, and wetlands for foraging and hunting, they established a village within sight of the twin knobs.

Sanderson reports in Graham (1883) that the "village contained 100 wigwams," while Scott (1877) estimated that the population was approximately "500 souls." For Chief Tarhe, the tall, charismatic leader of the Wyandot people, the infusion of white settlers probably seemed to start as a slow trickle, with traders initially bringing useful items. Later, these settlers became known to him not as traders but as poachers and squatters on the Wyandot territories. War broke out in 1774 as white cruelty to Chief Logan's family of the Mingo led to Dunmore's War. Along with other tribes, Chief Tarhe and the Wyandot people fought the white settlers at Point Pleasant in the fall of 1774. This war terminated with a signed treaty on the banks of the Scioto River, meant to guarantee the peoples a quiet place forever. Sadly, Allen and Ruble were a lot closer to lasting forever than the treaty of Camp Charlotte.

After the treaty, the area was quiet while the Revolutionary War between the Anglo Europeans raged to the east. Perhaps Chief Tarhe thought it ironic that Lord Dunmore and Colonel

Lewis, allies only a couple of years earlier, were now bitter enemies. The regional peace would not last long, however. These soon-to-be Americans from Pennsylvania and Virginia, perhaps struggling to farm in the rocky and steep hillsides of the east, got a glimpse of the rich, glaciated lands beyond the twin knobs during Dunmore's War. The treaty signed on the banks of the Scioto would soon become worthless.

At that time, as long as the Native Americans held control over an area, Anglo-Europeans could not occupy the ground. Following the American Revolution, three military campaigns against the Native Americans in Ohio resulted in disaster for the American militia-based armies. However, each battle weakened the Native Americans. Raids and counterraids across the Ohio River injured families, burned villages, and destroyed crops. Creative destruction was in progress. The Battle of Fallen Timbers that took place in 1794, fought by the American army, settled the matter. Chief Tarhe moved his people away from what would become Lancaster, Ohio, under the terms of the 1795 Treaty of Greenville. They left their homes in the Hocking area for new treaty lands around modern-day Sandusky.

Ebenezer Zane[11] cut his "trace," or early road, just to the south of the twin knobs, and Americans started to pour in. Scott (1877, pg. 5) reports that "in April 1798, Capt. Joseph Hunter, a bold and enterprising man, with his family, emigrated from Kentucky and settled on Zanes' Trace, upon the bank of the prairie west of the crossings…" Captain Hunter and his family

---

11 Zane was commissioned by congress in 1796 to mark a trail suitable for horseback from Wheeling, West Virginia, to Maysville, Kentucky.

were not without neighbors for very long. In 1798, Nathaniel Wilson arrived with his family and others to settle what would one day be Lancaster and the areas near the knobs. By the time that Jonathan Scofield arrived with his surveying crew in 1800, William Wilson was already raising wheat on a prairie south of the knobs. In 1817, Nathaniel Wilson set aside some land to the east of Shallenberger as a family burial ground, which would one day become a burial ground for American presidents. In 1838, his religious convictions led him to erect a twelve-sided sandstone wall, the same way the first temple was assembled in Jerusalem. The rock was shaped on-site at the knobs and transported to the cemetery to be dry fitted together without the loud sounds of construction. Although Nathaniel passed away before the project could be finished, his son, Gustin, finished it for him. The structure is probably the best example of dry fitted masonry in the country and today is part of the Fairfield County Park system.

Allen and Ruble felt the full force of Wilson's desire to build the structure. The drill holes, marked by red arrows in the photo on page 28, are about two inches in diameter. Under the pressure of the workmen's efforts to shape the rock, coupled with the movement of animals, the knobs and slopes must have been shaved bald by the finish of the cemetery. It is unclear whether all the quarrying was done just by the Wilson family for the cemetery. Perhaps it is unfair and inaccurate to assign to one family and project the removal of so much stone from the brother and sister knobs, since many buildings in Lancaster show sandstone construction.

*An aerial view from Google Earth illustrating the proximity
of Stonewall Cemetery to Shallenberger.*

Drill holes on Allen Knob. Photo courtesy of Judd Clover.

Photo courtesy of Judd Clover.

Look closely at the shadows in the photograph on page 30. The pit that is visible in the picture is found in the middle of Allen Knob. As the trail around the knob moves to the west, the pit will come into view. It is believed that Wilson quarried the capstone for Stonewall Cemetery from here, since the surface layer of Black Hand Sandstone is harder than the underlying layers due to longer contact with the seawater that glued the grains of sand together as the rock formed.

Chief Tarhe did not know what happened to Allen and Ruble Knobs, as he died in 1818 near the Sandusky River before the cemetery was started. By the time Wilson finished, only the Wyandots remained of the Native Americans that had lived in Ohio on treaty lands. Perhaps it was fortunate that Chief Tarhe passed on and did not endure the various land cessions that were agreed to

Photo courtesy of Judd Clover.

in response to white encroachment. Hurt (1998) describes a series of treaties that took place, each demanding a little more land from the Wyandot, right up until their sad departure from the state in 1843. The Wyandot departure was significant, as it denoted the end of the Pre-Settlement Era in Ohio as the last smoke from council fires forever disappeared into the Ohio sky.

Back on Allen and Ruble Knobs, the work was done. In the resulting rubble covering the slopes around the knobs, plants began to find their way back. Sprigs of green from seeds of maple, ash, tulip poplar, and elms sprang to life and found passage through the broken and discarded sandstone littering the sides. A remnant population of native wildflowers did what the Wyandot people could not do: escape notice until it was safe to re-emerge among the crags and rocks of the sibling knobs. With them, other wildflowers, some exotic strangers, found a foothold in the man-made disturbance, having long been accustomed to the ways of domestic animals and the steel of Europe and Asia.

On the gentler slopes below the shattered crowns, the business of felling trees continued. In the bright sunlight both north and south of the knobs, other native wildflowers and shrubs continued to disappear as European plants growing in pastures and cornfields pushed them aside.

European land philosophies, vastly different than those of the Native Americans, had arrived on the knobs. A new age dawned on the land: no longer would ice be the major catalyst of change, nor the sharp incisors of beavers, or even the flint tools of the Native Americans. The booming powder cracking rock, the pounding thuds of chisels and the moving of large cut stones showcased the full reality of European metal tools, domestic animals, and technology.

The rubble field left below Allen Knob after the quarry. Ironically, the loose rock may have protected native wildflowers such as trillium from deer predation.

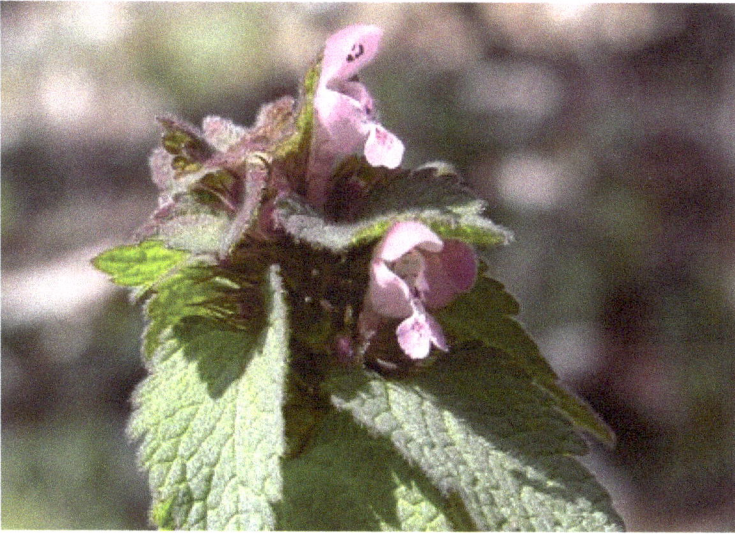

Purple dead nettle (Lamium purpureum) found during the winter
and spring on the south-facing slope of Allen Knob. This Eurasian
immigrant blooms early in the spring and summer.

The tanager has to sing louder now, the quiet is gone,
the storm still eddies around them while the Scotsman lies quietly
in his cemetery of stone he stole from the brother and sister…

Though ageless, the two siblings are tattered and worn,
having endured the tides of ice and men.

And time marches on…

Zane's Trace eventually morphed into a larger road, and horses made way for automobiles and trucks. Over the years, as the knobs re-grew their forests, traffic shifted from hay and corn-fueled vehicles to those using petrochemical combustion, causing the noise levels to rise. State Route 22 on the south boundary of Shallenberger continued to shuttle the traffic between Circleville and Lancaster to which it had been accustomed long before the site was dedicated.

State Route 33 carried most of the northern and southern traffic between Columbus and Athens right through the middle of Lancaster. Both commuter and commercial traffic became intolerable, with Memorial Drive, which passes through town, better resembling a parking lot than a thoroughfare. The concept of creative destruction emerges again in the shape of the eventual construction of a limited-access highway through the farmland to the west, allowing traffic to go faster. The bypass was completed in 2005.

View from Allen Knob to the southwest; the intersection of US 22 and US 33.

With the help of Google Maps, a couple of interesting thoughts emerge from this development. At the closest point, US Route 33 passes by a parking lot 1,200 feet away to the west. US Route 22 is found about the same distance south of the Shallenberger Preserve parking lot. The intersection in the photo on page 34 is near the preserve parking lot. Traffic noise from both highways is audible throughout the preserve. Almost a mile due east of the preserve, away from the bypass and in a quiet, exurban neighborhood, lies the Wilson family, "quietly" settled in Stonewall Cemetery.

The impact of various forces on the twin knobs continues, not from glaciers, gun powder, or drills, but from an economic construct with unintended consequences: the Columbian Exchange. Named for Christopher Columbus, the arrival of Anglo Europeans into North America brought European-Asian plants, animals and diseases. Unfortunately, this trading of organisms, both beneficial and harmful, extended both ways across the ocean and eventually to all continents. With much more rapidly spreading consequences than the glaciers, this force carries the seeds of change from far-off places, flowing through and over the knobs effortlessly. Almost unnoticed until it was too late, this invasion quickly began to reconstruct both forest and field into a botanical copy of Europe and Asia.

THE FOREST:
YESTERDAY AND TODAY

TO WALK ACROSS the grassy strip from the Shallenberger parking lot onto the trail creates a sense of passing through an opening into another dimension.

The dedication plaque at the entrance takes on a new significance as a wall of trees greets the hiker.

A young forest dominated by small sugar maple and black cherry trees greets the visitor. The forked tree in the foreground of

After the thunder, the trees came creeping back, but the mighty chestnut was lost forever.

the picture on page 37 is a black cherry (*Prunus serotina).* Black cherry trees sprout easily, and along with other successional species start the process of raising up a forest from a field. Until its dedication in 1973, the land in this image was an open field. In the Shallenberger Preserve Management Plan, the Primary Management Goal listed is "to perpetuate and enhance forest communities." The preserve is well on its way to achieving this goal, with a couple of reservations.

As the land has recovered from its previous abuse, the forest has changed from an oak- to a maple-dominated forest. Foreign diseases and insects have also seriously impacted the chestnut, elm, and ash trees that populate the preserve. Despite the historical assaults of the land by saws and continued plagues, passage

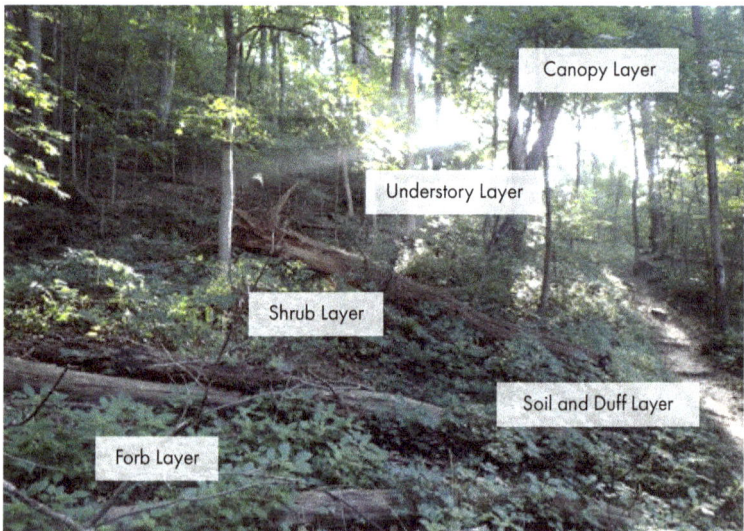

The view while climbing up the south side of Allen Knob in the morning. The labels attempt to illustrate the above ground layers formed by different height classes of plants.

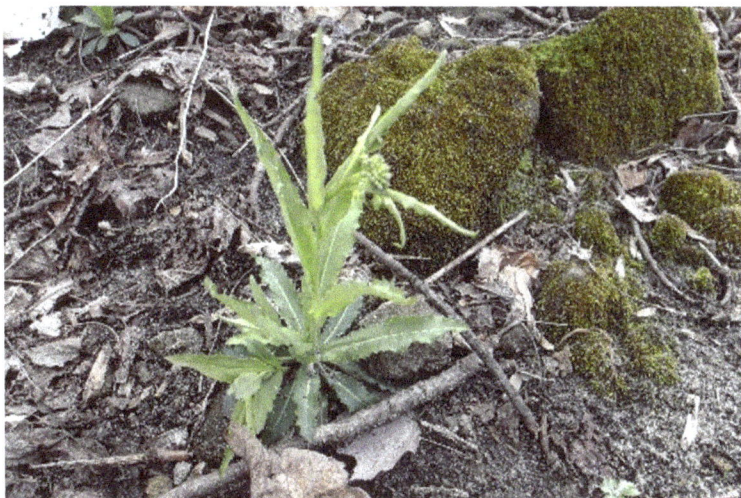

The twigs and dead leaves belong to the duff layer, right above the soil surrounding the smooth rockcress on the south slope of Allen Knob. The rockcress, in turn, belongs to the forb layer.

through the preserve reveals the success of the plan, as trees have returned and blanketed the area.

Nature in its raw form is a bit foreign to most folks, as the forest has a different and perhaps unfamiliar style of organization. One can start to unravel a natural area by looking at the photo on page 38 as a series of layers and a function of time. Within the established forest, starting with the bottom soil and duff layer, species of vegetation, depending on mature height, form layers. From the ground, plants grow upward and stop with the forb layer, shrub layer, understory and finally on top, the canopy layer. Time factors into the process as shrubs and trees grow and emerge from the forb layer into higher layers. Age is a primary determinant as a bare field recovers slowly through the years into a forest, a process termed succession.

The smooth rockcress in the photo on page 39 is on the south side of Allen Knob and illustrates the sandy soil that lies at the foot of the knobs. Eroding bedrock, glacially moved material, and organic matter form soil over the bedrock below. The duff layer[12] is found right on top of the soil and intermingles with it, similar to fallen leaves and sticks. As duff decays, it adds to the organic portion of the soil. The forb layer [13]contains wildflowers, grasses, and sedges. Young trees and shrubs break through this layer as they grow taller. We will revisit and discuss the forb layer in chapter five.

The shrub layer is where plants can get a little confusing. They may be small, but they have woody stems. Young trees pass through the shrub layer as they grow, while plants such as spice bush, mountain laurel, viburnum, and gooseberry stay there. Foreign invaders in the shrub layer at Shallenberger include honeysuckle, multiflora rose, and privet. Japanese Barberry is also present in very small amounts. A later chapter, Protecting the Remnants, will discuss foreign invading plants in more detail.

The shrub layer is important for pollinators, browsers, and birds alike. Some shrub layer species grow to be approximately as tall as an adult human, while others, like the lowbush blueberries found along the rims of the knobs, may not grow more than knee-high.

The understory sits right under the canopy. Key players in this layer include hop hornbeam, paw paws, service berry, and

12 Duff is composed of dead leaves, sticks, decaying wood, dead animals and other = materials that were once alive.

13 A common term for "forb" is "weed." Another definition of this term is a plant without a woody stem.

flowering dogwood. These species, similar to the shrub layer, are able to live in the dappled sunshine that descends through the leaves above. Canopy trees pass through this layer as they grow, stretching and reaching for the sky. Some species of canopy trees, such as maple and beech, may spend their lives in this layer, waiting for a larger neighbor to die or fall so they can have their opportunity to shoot toward the sun. In the image on page 43, the canopy can be found at the very top.

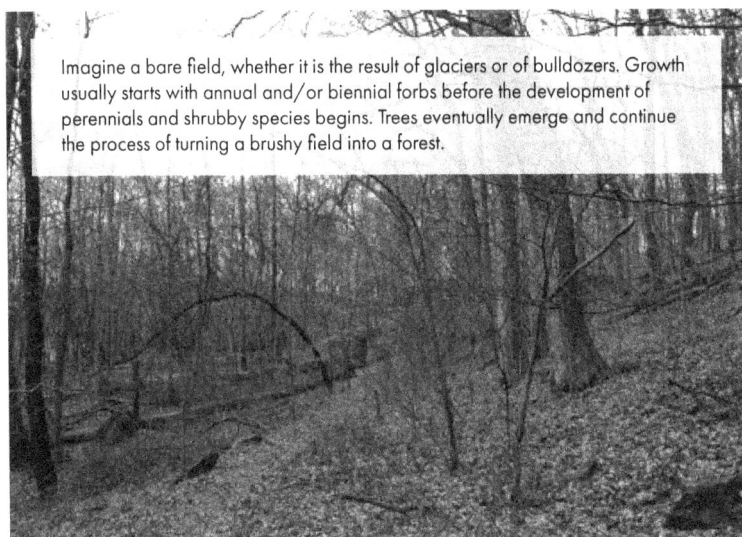

Imagine a bare field, whether it is the result of glaciers or of bulldozers. Growth usually starts with annual and/or biennial forbs before the development of perennials and shrubby species begins. Trees eventually emerge and continue the process of turning a brushy field into a forest.

Looking down the trail on Allen Knob with the parking lot in the distance. Compare the sizes of the trees on the left and right sides of the trail. The area on the left side of the photo was used for crops or pasture until the dedication of the preserve, but the trees on the right show evidence of coming from an older forest.

The photo above illustrates two adjacent forests of differing ages. This is the result of succession. Succession is a function of time and varies depending on the plants available in the area. Vegetation progresses from one state to another, with various species coming and going until the area reaches a mature state. Ohio, along with adjoining states, is classified as part of the Eastern Temperate Forest. E. Lucy Braun (1989) writes, "the State of Ohio, containing about 40,000 square miles was once a magnificent hardwood forest." This quote suggests that the mature or end state of succession in Ohio would be that of a "magnificent hardwood forest."

The west side of Allen Knob. The blooming tree is serviceberry (Amelanchier arborea). Notice the anchor point of this tree is near the bottom of the cliff. Serviceberry can attain a maximum height of 50 feet and is an understory tree. Anchored on the cliff top, the plant with green leaves in the foreground is mountain laurel (Kalmia latifolia), a shrub with a maximum height of twelve to fifteen feet. A young, smooth-barked beech is visible behind the serviceberry and the dark chestnut oak on the right, are ascending into the canopy layer.

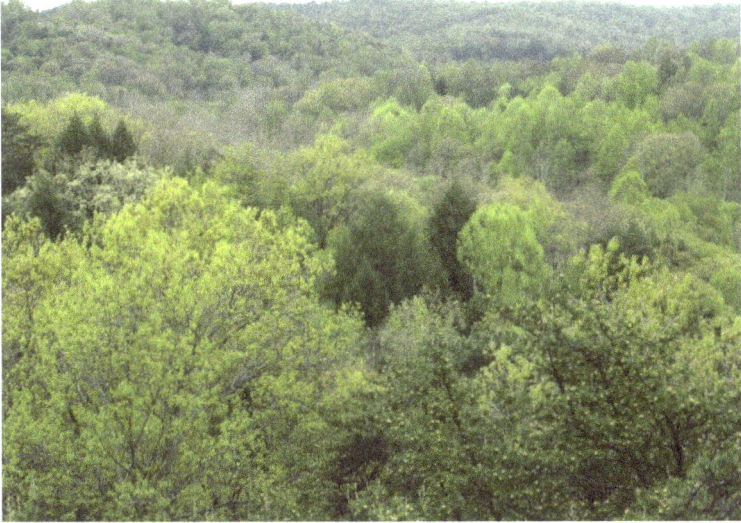

Another view of the canopy layer from the top.

Bush honeysuckle, Lonicera maackii, a shrub layer invader. November 29, 2023.

The great forest spreading across the physiographic regions of Ohio and creeping up the knobs was a "magnificent" biome.[14] Punctuated by prairies and wetlands, it became a rich habitat for animals and humans alike. However, the forest that was thousands of years in the making would eventually disappear in less than a hundred years.

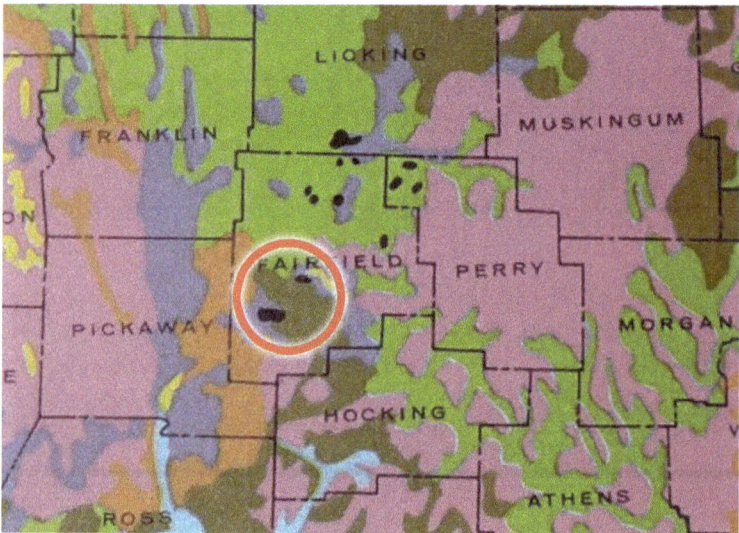

The different colors depict the merging of mixed oak forests (pink) with beech (green), mixed mesophytic (brown), and elm ash swamp (blue). The yellow sliver represents a prairie region. The light tannish-brown represents the presence of an oak sugar maple-dominated forest. Notice the mixing of forest type communities in this portion of Fairfield County, which contains Shallenberger. Map from Robert Gordon, 1969.

---

14 Biome: a biological gathering of species that require the same climate and topography. Think of deserts, prairies, rainforests, or tundras. Each represents a biome. Biomes, in turn, can be divided into communities that form within more restricted areas, such as the different forest types illustrated above.

*Section statements from the Hocking Township Survey (Scofield 1800).
It is copied verbatim over a 1:24,000 topographic map in the next
illustration. From Scofield, Jonathan. 1800. "Township North 14, Range
North 19." Ohio Historical Society. Notice Scofield (or a team member
writes "across the prairie to William Wilson's wheat field." Look for that
comment in the lower left on the illustration on page 46.*

In a 1969 study, Robert Gordon plotted this map based
on his book, *The Natural Vegetation of Ohio in Pioneer Days*. The
different forests, as later explored by the geologist Jane Forsyth
(1970), formed over soils influenced by bedrock and glaciers. The
close proximity of Black Hand Sandstone and the Appalachian
Plateau, coupled with the glaciated and unglaciated areas around
Shallenberger, resulted in the meeting of four different forest types.

Charles Gordon (1969) and Jane Forsyth (1970) both had
previous historical data to help them in their work. In 1799
and 1800, surveyors crossed the county in response to the
Land Ordinance of 1785 and the 1787 Northwest Ordinance
(Knepper, 2002).[15] They marked and organized the Ohio territory

15 Adena Museum in Chillicothe has on exhibit the equipment used by the surveyors.
The bibliography contains the reference information for Jane Forsyth, Robert Gordon and
George Knepper.

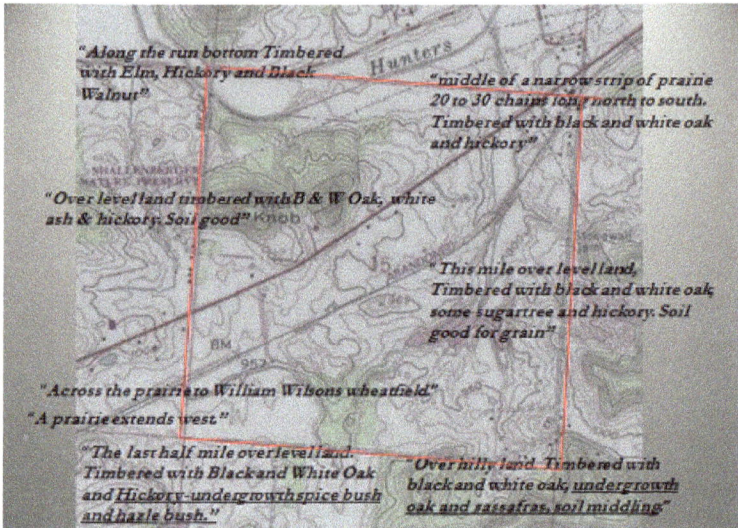

This illustration depicts section statements overlaid on a 1:24,000 scale topographical map for section 15 of Fairfield County. Allen and Ruble are in the upper left corner. The map is from "Topo" Outdoor Recreation Mapping Software by National Geographic.

into uniform sections. At section corners, two trees were blazed as witness trees. The species of trees in each section were recorded, along with their direction and distance from the witness point. The surveyors also wrote short descriptions of each area, or section statements, to describe the land they had just crossed.

Analyzing these surveys has assisted researchers to partially recreate the pre-settlement forest; there are, however, pitfalls to watch out for when using this method. At the time, the federal government had needed the revenues from the sale of these lands, and the surveyors were paid for each section of land surveyed. Gordon (1969) also argues that the selection of witness trees "was more or less arbitrary." For the purposes of this discussion, section statements, rather than witness trees, are more useful in determining a snapshot of the pre-settlement forest composition around the twin knobs.

The illustration on page 46 contains the italicized section statements from the survey of section (15), which surrounds Shallenberger State Nature Preserve. The red lines are the boundaries of this section, which was surveyed by Jonathan Scofield's crew. These statements were probably written by Scofield or a crew member. In the illustration the statements are placed over the corresponding section of ground aligned on a modern topographic map. By the time of the survey in 1800, which included the area around the knobs, Anglo European changes were already taking place, as evidenced by the presence of a wheat field noted in Scofield's (1800) section notes. Wheat did not exist in Ohio prior to arrival of Europeans.

Gordon (1969) reports that the "most widespread at the time of the earliest land surveys were forests containing white oaks, black oaks, and some species of hickory." The rest of Fairfield County was similar. Analyzing section statements from the entire county revealed the following percentages of forest types:

White Oak, Black Oak, Hickory Association	62%
Oak, Sugar Maple Association	22%
Elm Ash Swamp Forests, wet Prairie	8%
Prairie, Glades	14%
Hazlenut understory	9%
Oak Brush	16%

Fairfield County contains glaciated and unglaciated areas. Referencing chapter two, three physiographic regions border each other within the county. Each region brings its own complement of forest types. According to the surveyor comments on the image on page 46, at the time of the survey, oaks dominated the section where Fairfield County is currently located. The comment, "over level land," on the west side seems incongruous with the steep relief that is indicated by the map. This is especially true since the surveying party moved along the line on the map that corresponds with Becks Knob Road along the western boundary of the preserve, which does present with a rise and descent. However, the party had moved westward from the unglaciated and more steeply dissected hills east of that point, so the relief around the knobs probably did seem level to them.

This chart contains a count of the individual witness trees recorded across Hocking Township.

December 1800

Compare the graph on page 48 (December 1800) with the one below (Present Day Shallenberger). The left-most bars that are circled in red are white oak and black oak, followed by hickory. The percentages of oaks and hickories from the original Hocking Township survey contrast sharply with the percentages found in the Present Day graph, in which the maples, circled in blue, as well as some other varieties, such as tulip poplars, dominate the graph, representing the populations now seen at Shallenberger. There seems to have been a rapid shift from oak-dominated to maple-dominated forests.

Present Day Shallenberger

The data in these graphs supports George Augustus Heffner's conclusion in his 1939 master's thesis analyzing forest remnants in Fairfield County, in which he states, "At present there are only a few woodlots that may contain original forest trees." All across the county, the forest had changed. It had occurred within the short time span of a few human generations, which indicates that it cannot be blamed on glaciers or asteroids.

The data in these charts was comprised of trees counted throughout the trail system that could be touched from the midline of the trail. Referring back to the illustration on page 46, Jonathan Scofield wrote of the west side of the section, "over level land timbered with B & W Oak, white ash and hickory, Soil good." The background photo in the chart above ironically illustrates a line of large sugar maples, rather than oaks, found on the west side of Allen Knob along the same line about which Jonathan Scofield wrote those comments in 1800. Faced by this role reversal between oaks and maples, the question arises, what happened?

The answer is simple: the forest was cleared. At first, pioneer settlers girdled the trees to open land for farming. From 1850 on, timber was cleared commercially to use on railroads, in the coal mines of Perry County, and later on, oil derricks. The Preserve Manager with volunteer Judd Clover conducted the following annual[16] ring counts to measure the age of ash trees that had been cut down in 2016: 117, 127, 111, 105, 110, 110, and 144. This is not exactly a complete statistical analysis of the current forest age, but the ages of these ash trees support the idea that trees on the knobs began to recover around the turn of the century.

A possible reason for this relates to vanished Native American populations that used to live in the area. Due the loss of Native Americans, fire ceased to influence forests around the knobs. Oaks,

---

16 Each year a tree or shrub forms a new layer of water conducting cells termed xylem tissue. The age of these large ash trees that had become infected by emerald ash borer and died indicated they had sprouted around both sides of 1900.

being somewhat resistant to fire, had previously enjoyed the release from competition that periodic fires brought to the woodlands, causing their populations to flourish. When the fires were less prevalent, this advantage was gone, so once the oaks were cut and without the presence of fire, maple, tulip poplar, and ash trees could reseed the area with younger trees. Oaks were on the decrease.

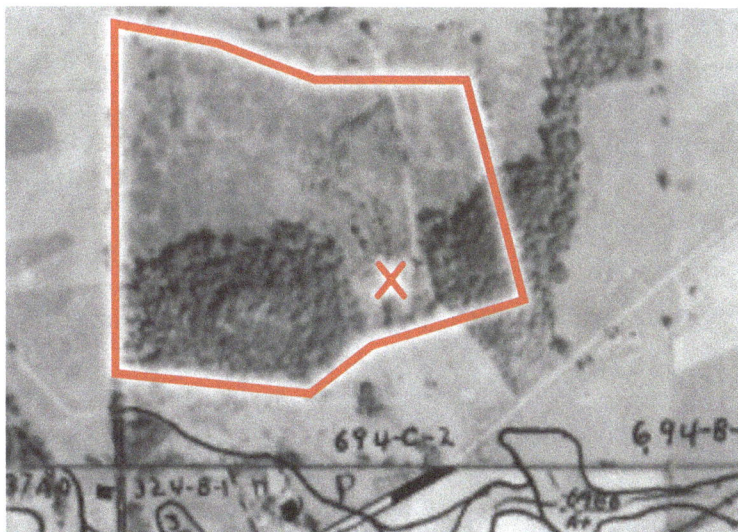

Aerial photo from 1938. Courtesy of Christina Holt of Fairfield Soil and Water Conservation District and Rob Myers of the Department of Natural Areas and Preserves. Allen Knob is on the left and Ruble Knob is on the right, with the modern-day area of the preserve outlined in red. The approximate position of the barbed wire found in the photograph on page 53 is marked by an "X" on the southern boundary of the preserve.

The aerial photo above provides some additional clues to the reason for the shift in tree populations. At the time when this photograph was taken, both knobs appeared to be wooded, while the land both north and south of the knobs appeared to be cleared.

The rougher texture of the area around the knobs contrasts with the smoother-appearing croplands surrounding the site. The barbed wire and the texture of the land found in the picture on the next page provides clues that suggest that the area around the knobs may have been pasture that had begun to slip into a shrubby succession before the photo above was taken. Other clues that can be seen today include armored, thorny shrubs, such as the invasive multiflora rose and native gooseberry, plants that proliferate over grazed sites because animals avoid the thorns.

The forest did return, eventually. Probably not due to the "benign neglect" of Wallace's sandstone ridge, but to the steep topography of the knobs and the actions of farsighted individuals such as Jay Shallenberger who placed this property into preservation. Sadly, the forest that returned was not the same one that had disappeared, but the observant hiker can still find some remaining giants from the past.

"The forests of southeastern Ohio differ markedly from the regional forest of only 200 years ago [...] Oak and Hickory have decreased in abundance, while sugar maple and red maple have increased." Dyer, 2001

For the purposes of this story, it is necessary to concede that the surveyor from the 1800 report did not identify all the trees that are significant to Allen and Ruble, both yesterday and today. If a species was not listed in the 1800 report, it does not mean that it was not there. The numbers of tulip poplar, hackberry, chestnut oak, and other native species in southeast Ohio readily defy that thought.

Allis Sawtooth barbed wire embedded in a sugar maple. This wire was possibly used during the late 1800s. Photo courtesy of Rob Myers.

For example, Chestnut oaks (*Quercus prinus*) were not mentioned in the survey. By contrast, Braun (1989) describes them as "A tree of the Appalachian Highlands and non-calcareous sections of the interior low plateau." As is found everywhere along the ridges in the Appalachian plateau, chestnut oaks are currently prevalent on the south-facing slope of Allen Knob, around its rocky edges, and dominating the ridge on Ruble Knob, overtaking the tulip poplar and maple as the knob rises.

Hackberry and the less common hop hornbeams (pictured on page 56) leave to conjecture what their population density was during the time Jonathan Scofield surveyed area the knobs. Both species are a common presence in the preserve today. Once considered to be in the same genus as elms (Ulmus) and very comfortable growing on the moist lower slopes, perhaps the hack-berry were misidentified as elms, hence their absence in the historical record.

The presence of black gum (*Nyssa sylvatica*) was recorded in the 1800 survey. It raises an interesting observation, though it is probably a coincidence, rather than anything terribly scientific: the bumps representing the population of these trees in 1800 are about the same size as those on the original township survey, as well as the trail survey and the population common in the preserve today. Along the trail, large black gums stand out by the alligator skin like bark and are surrounded by a miniature thicket of deer-grazed root sprouts about knee-high.

White and green ash became dominant species within the maturing forest after the disappearance of oaks, but they are quickly

Chestnut oaks facing south on Allen Knob.

losing their importance over time. A walk around the preserve today reveals many dying and fallen ash trees that are the victims of disease.

Looking east from Allen Knob toward Ruble Knob. The various trunk diameters are evidence of a maturing forest.

Shallenberger contained a large population of white ash,[17] but also has some green ash and a few blue ash. The giant blue ash illustrated on page 58 lies below the trail on the northwest side of Allen Knob, where it fell in 2022. Blue ash is mostly found near the north and west boundaries of Shallenberger, and exists "where glacial soils are calcareous." (Braun, 1989). This soil is the result of past glacial activity: as the glacier pushed up against the knobs and started to melt, lime-laden soils from the western and northern

---

17 The scientific name of white ash is Fraxinus americana, green ash is F. pennsylvanica, and blue ash is Fraximus quadrangulata. Ohio also has two other species of ash that are found outside of Fairfield County. All species of ash are in danger of loss due to the activities of the emerald ash borer.

The sassafras pictured above (Sassafras albidum), an early successional tree, is aging out of the maturing forest.

Hop hornbeam (Ostrya virginiana) is an understory tree that is well-adapted to the acidic, rocky soils of Shallenberger.

parts of the state were dropped against the northern slopes as part of a glacial moraine. Despite the presence of the acidic sandstone, enough lime was there to encourage the growth of lime-loving plants including the blue ash.

Hackberry (Celtis occidentalis). On the moist soils along the lower slopes of the knobs, these trees are doing well. The unique warty bark enables fairly easy identification of these trees, even when the leaves are not visible. Their fall fruits serve birds well. Notice that the invasive honeysuckle shrub in the right rear foreground still has leaves.

Native to Asia, in 2003, the emerald ash borer arrived in Ohio and started attacking native ash trees. With lightning speed, the emerald ash borer arrived at Shallenberger and wreaked total havoc on the populations there. The arrival of the ash borer and destruction of ash trees at Shallenberger did not take place over forest time, or even a single human generation, but within a few years. This invasive species destroys trees in the following manner:

The emerald ash borer larva attacks and devours the cambium layer within the tree, similar to weed whipping a shrub and killing it.

A large blue ash recently fallen on the northwest side of Allen Knob along the trail. The blue ash presence in the preserve, usually found on higher pH soils, is a product of glacial soils resting against the slopes.

Despite the destruction of the trees by the emerald ash borer, young ash trees are still common in the shrub and forb layers, with surviving[18] female ash trees producing abundant winged seeds that germinate well. The young trees are largely unmolested by the beetles until they reach about 2.5 inches in diameter before the beetles begin to attack. As the trail swings around to the east on the northwest side of Allen Knob, many three-to-five-foot sprouts of white ash, like the ones in the photo below, come into view.

---

18 Ash trees are dioicous meaning that separate trees contain either all male or all female flowers. Male trees produce pollen. Female trees produce seeds after the flowers are pollinated.

The agonizing hope for a natural enemy to the borer to appear is dwindling as the time passes.

Years before the emerald ash borer arrived, the Dutch elm disease also wreaked havoc across the nation on both the American elm (*Ulmus americana*) and red elm (*Ulmus rubra*) species. The large red elm tree in the photo on page 61 has succumbed to the Dutch elm disease. Notice how the bark has fallen off and lays at the bottom of the tree. In the Dutch elm disease, one of two fungal pathogens spread into the tree by elm bark beetles destroy the cambium layer. Though the mechanism between the elm and ash are different, the result is the same, with the cambium layer destroyed, the tree cannot circulate nutrients and water and dies. The emerald ash borer and the Dutch elm disease are responsible for many of the large dead tree skeletons now sinking into the forest floor across the midwest.

Collection of young ash sprouts along the trail on the northwest side of Allen Knob.

The dangers to the forest are not limited to non-native diseases: wind is a problem on the knobs due to the unlimited exposure and shallow soil. The Preserve Management Plan also references an ice storm in 1988 that damaged many of the trees on Allen Knob. DNAP staff and volunteers constantly monitor the trails for windfalls. In the image below, preserve staff are cutting away a large red oak that fell across a newly constructed footbridge in June of 2015.

The natural loss of great trees to wind or disease is a sad but essential part of the cycle of life in a forest. Fallen or dead wood is not removed in a nature preserve but left to the most important members of the food chain: the decomposers.[19] At the right time of year, the forest floor of the preserve can literally light up from

19 Decomposers turn dead things such as animals, branches, leaves, and waste, such as poop, back into soil. Several species across a spectrum of bacteria, insects, and fungi help with this important job. A saprobe is a decomposer that obtains its nutrients from dead and decomposing organic matter, i.e. dead wood and leaves.

Large Elm that succumbed to Dutch elm disease. This tree has since fallen but can be seen lying perpendicular to the trail below Allen Knob.

A native bee, possibly a halictid, making her home in fallen tree trunk. April 13, 2015.

These trees stand out because of their size and their large lower limbs that are thick and heavy, pushing out through the younger trees beside them. They are from another age. The large lower limbs tell us that at one time they were lone trees, survivors spared from the sawmill. Growing in the sun of a pasture or at the edge of a field allowed them to spread their lower limbs. Look for this old giant along the trail below and east of Ruble Knob.

Old white oaks at Shallenberger provide a glimpse into the past.

The oaks form a rough line toward the west, including the white oak on the preceding page. Notice how smaller, younger trees surround the older oaks. When the area to the north of the knobs was first cleared, these oaks were young trees, possibly left to mark a property or fence line. Like the white oak on the preceding page, they were probably surrounded by cropland or pasture.

Large white oaks on the southern slope of Ruble Knob on the downhill side of the trail.

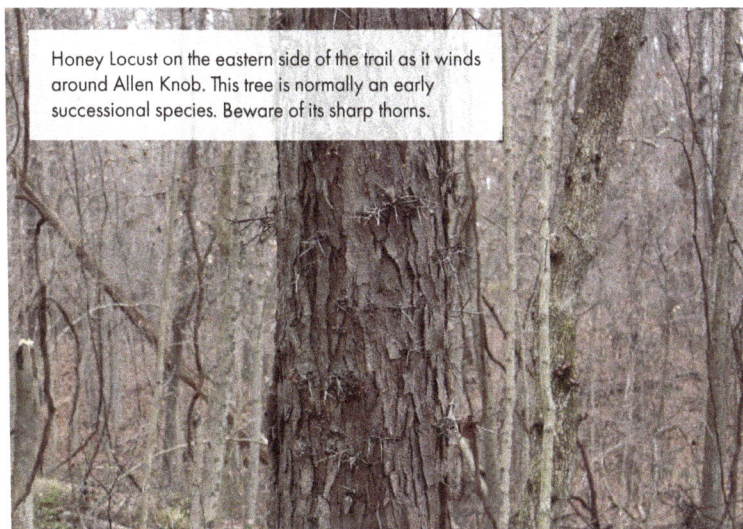

Honey Locust on the eastern side of the trail as it winds around Allen Knob. This tree is normally an early successional species. Beware of its sharp thorns.

Honey locust tree (Gleditsia triacanthos).

Perhaps they were there all along with the combined oak and sugar maple-dominated forest hovering to the west and north. Gordon's original vegetation map of Ohio (1969) confirms that this oak and sugar maple-dominated forest ran right up into Fairfield County.

Sugar maple has the ability to patiently wait in the shade of other trees before taking advantage of an opening in the canopy and racing upward. The paired winged samaras are able to flutter long distances through the fall woods and grab space as it opens up.

This maple is on the west side of the preserve, sandwiched between the trail and Beck's Knob Road. This tree's thick, perpendicular lower limbs harken back to a time when it grew by itself in a pasture or hayfield.

For a map of Ohio's original vegetation check out *The Natural Vegetation of Ohio, at the Time of the Earliest Land Surveys*, by Robert B. Gordon, Ohio Biological Survey, 1966 at Gordon's Natural Vegetation of Ohio Map – Building Ohio State (osu.edu)

Today, sugar maple (Acer saccharum) has become the prevalent tree on and around the knobs.

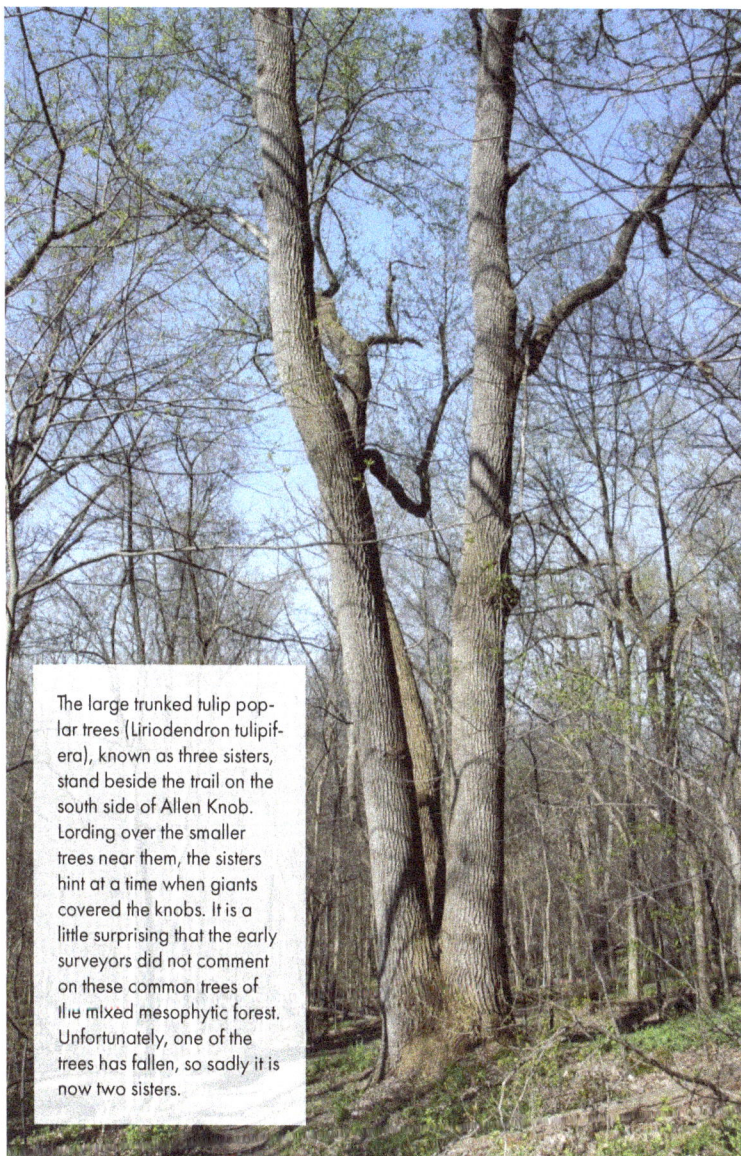

The large trunked tulip poplar trees (Liriodendron tulipifera), known as three sisters, stand beside the trail on the south side of Allen Knob. Lording over the smaller trees near them, the sisters hint at a time when giants covered the knobs. It is a little surprising that the early surveyors did not comment on these common trees of the mixed mesophytic forest. Unfortunately, one of the trees has fallen, so sadly it is now two sisters.

The three sisters, grand matriarchs of the preserve.

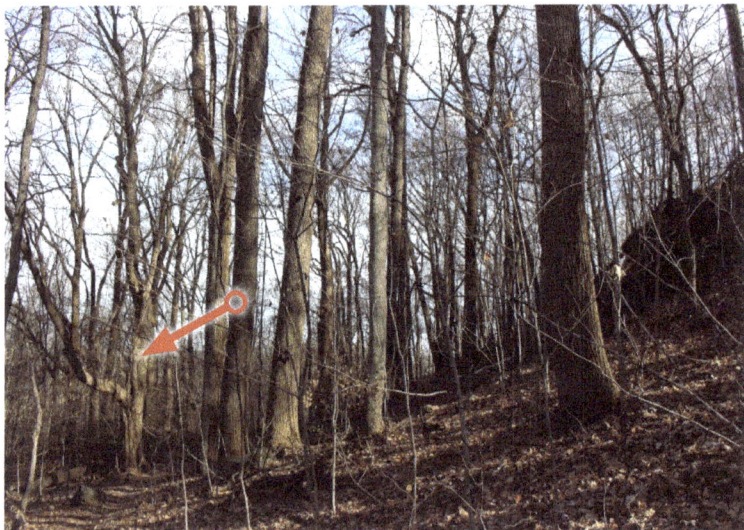

Maturing tulip poplars dominating the north side of Allen Knob on the uphill side above the trail. Notice the old sugar maple (indicated by the red arrow) that was here long before the tulip poplars reforested this slope.

From the genus *Laetiporus*, several similar species of mushrooms known as "sulfur shelf" or "chicken of the woods" assist in decomposing fallen wood. Visible in the photo is the fruiting body. In decomposition, the saprophytic threads of the fungus run through the wood and assist other decomposers in breaking down the old tree trunk for to be recycled by the forest.

Often found hanging on the underside of a log, the coral tooth fungus (*Hericium carolloides*) is also a saprobe. By contrast, the elf cup (*Sarcosphylla*), pictured on page 68, is an early spring saprobe that digests dead wood in the duff or soil layer. This fungus begins fruiting about the same time that the first wildflowers start to color the knobs.

Sulfur Shelf. Picture courtesy of Judd Clover, August 2013.

Coral Tooth Fungus

Elf cups lying among the fallen leaves of chestnut oaks.

UNDER THE TREES

Tanagers sang happy songs from leafy perches while hepatica
and trillium dotted the dark soil with earthbound stars.

THE WILDFLOWER SHOW starts in late winter and early
spring. Flowers generally start opening up high on the southeastern
slopes. As spring progresses and the sun moves higher in the sky, the
flowers farther down the slopes begin to bloom. Hiking in the late
fall, winter, and early spring reveals the sun's influence on this preserve. The sun shining on the uphill climb feels good on the south

April 12, 2015. Walking fern, marginal wood fern, and hepatica
cling to a sandstone ledge on the north side of Allen Knob.

slope of Allen Knob on a cool day. If the hiker continues around to the north side of Allen Knob, it is certain that the sweater will go back on as the sun turns to shade. This hiker has experienced aspect. Aspect describes the ground's shape and relationship to the sun. The angle and amount of time the sun shines on the slope determines the amount of moisture in the ground, hence, the growth rate of the vegetation. Termed as insolation, it is a measure of solar energy (sunlight) as it impacts a square meter of ground. Imagine a bundle of sunlight the size of a square meter racing through space, hitting the leaves, and working its way to the ground.

The uphill aspect of the south slope enables sunlight to impact the soil and plants directly. The sun's impact on the north slope is more diffuse and less intense, consequently, the south

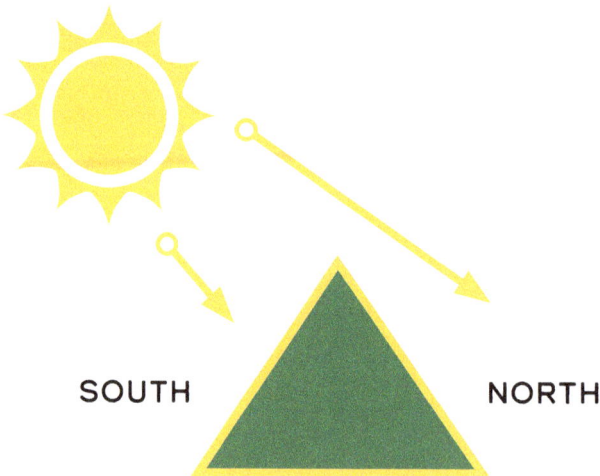

The impact of sunlight is more direct on the south side of the hill. In many cases, the south slope of hills across Ohio are drier than the north slope.

The amount of sunlight on the forest floor tells us that the spring wildflowers will be in bloom before the trees leaf out. Within a month, the trees will shade the ground.

Trail along the north side of Allen Knob in the spring.

Bloodroot (Sanguinaria canadensis) on the southeast slope of Allen Knob, an early bloomer.

slope is warmer and drier than the north slope. Approaching the summer solstice and beyond, the sun climbs higher in the sky and insolates the north slope by midsummer. By that time, most of the spring wildflowers have bloomed and died down while the trees and shrubs are fully leafed out.

In addition to the slope-driven relationship with the sun, the soil types formed by the bedrock and glaciation create different habitats for different plant communities. The deep soils along the north slope received direct contact with the glacier and a little more lime, while the soil around the top of the knob is shallow and more influenced by the acidic sandstone. Arguably, the most important reason that the many beautiful plants of Shallenberger Preserve cling to the knobs is stability. Historical pasturing or cropping on the slopes leading away from the knobs eliminated

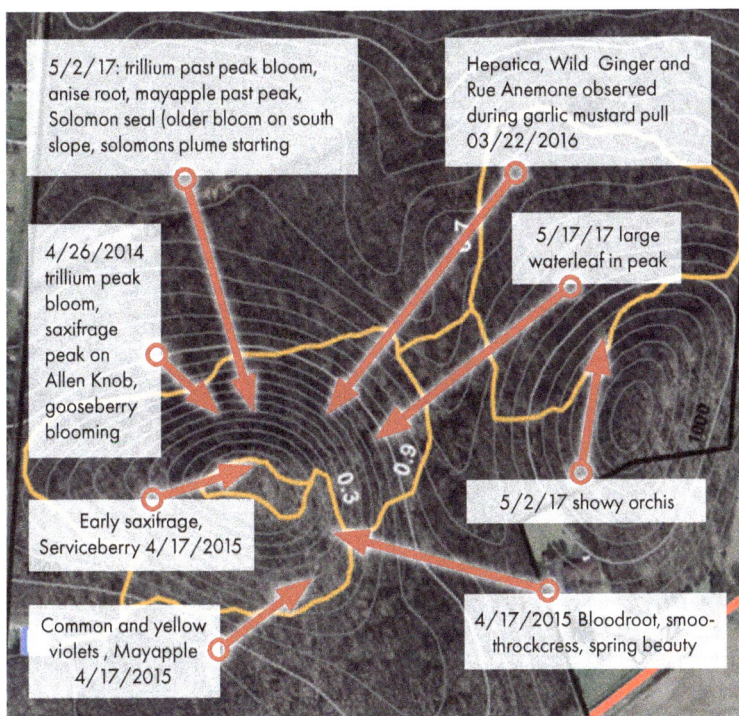

The Early Bloomers and locations: From the notebook of a previous preserve manager. These comments were made during garlic mustard pulls in the early spring. Steven Clements and Carol Gracie's book, Wildflowers in the Field and Forest (2006), provides the common names used here.

many native plants in those areas. The steep slopes of the knobs provided some protection from disturbance.

The trail photo on page 71 hints at the spectacular wildflower show that appears each spring. If a visitor looked upward into the trees when the picture was taken, they would notice that the buds of leaves and flowers on the trees are barely opening. Before the trees leaf out and shade the forest floor, spring ephemerals speed through their growth, reproduction, and energy storage. These plants, with their modified enzymes, are able to convert carbon dioxide, water, and nutrients into stored energy in their rhizomes, tubers, bulbs, and corms. The storage organs for these plants require stability. Plows, rototillers, logging, mowing, ATV traffic, and uncontrolled foot traffic all will destroy these plants.

Large flowered trillium (trillium grandiflorum).

Once the blooming is done, the ephemerals[20] fade away with the shading of the forest floor and wait patiently through another summer, fall, and winter before bursting out again. Many of these plants are long-lived perennials. In *Wildflowers in the Field and Forest,* Steven Clements and Carol Gracie report that trillium can live to an "excess of 70 years of age as determined by counting growth rings at the root collar."

---

20 The word ephemeral describes something that is here briefly and then goes away. Not all spring-blooming plants are ephemerals. For example, wild ginger and bloodroot retain their leaves through the summer and into early fall.

Many spring ephemerals have ant-dispersed seeds. These plants produce an oil body on the seed, an elaiosome, that induces ants to move the seed to their colonies. Once there, they eat the elaiosome and leave the seed in the rich, loose soil of the colony to grow. Sadly, trillium seeds have proven to have low viability and may not recover in clear-cut forests. Controlling non-native plants inside the trail loop around Allen Knob and on the south slope of Ruble Knob is a triage tactic for protecting the vulnerable native forbs on the slopes. Garlic mustard is a non-native invader, which will be discussed later, that impacts this area.

Trillium blooming in the rubble field below Allen Knob.

Trillium is often called "deer candy." Whitetail deer love to eat it and will graze out an entire population. In an ironic twist of fate, the rubble field that appeared from the quarrying of Allen

Knob may prove difficult for deer to walk in. Consequently, the trillium does well there.

Spring beauties and cut-leaved toothworts are true spring ephemerals and are very common around the twin knobs. Spring beauties grow very quickly, maturing from flowering to seed in two weeks and then dying shortly after to await the next spring.

Spring beauty (claytonia virginica).

Spring beauties serve insects by providing ants with elaiosomes from their seeds, enterprising mammals with their underground corms, and pollinators with nectar and pollen. Like many of the other forest forbs, this perennial has contractile roots that anchor the plant more securely with each season. Watch the flowers for the early flying andrena bees. Clements and Gracie report that over 100 different insects visit the flowers. Spring beauties seem to have weathered historical disturbance better than their native neighbors and do very well on the northern and western sides of Allen Knob. They dependably provide color on the bare spring ground.

Cut-leaved toothworts, like spring beauties, are true ephemerals and melt away after blooming. Toothworts are members of the mustard family, and they are related to the cabbage and broccoli found in our gardens. The spread of toothwort's European cousin, garlic mustard, has seriously affected a native butterfly, the West Virginia white, which pupates on toothworts. The adult female is attracted to the garlic mustard in place of the toothwort which then creates a toxic compound to the grazing caterpillar. Spring beauties and toothworts often can be found on the spur trail that leads to Allen Knob. As the season progresses, the southwest side of Allen Knob lights up with these flowers.

Cut-leaved toothwort (cardamine concatenata).

Bloodroot (sanguinaria canadensis). The blooms are short-lived, but the leaves will persist through the summer.

As the trail bends around the north sides of Allen and Ruble Knob, watch the dark, sandy soil for low, heart-shaped leaves. Around the time when hepatica starts blooming and spring beauties open, wild ginger also begins to bloom. The flowers may go unnoticed, as this plant hides its blooms well. Researchers are unsure exactly who pollinates this three-petaled flower.

23 March 2018:
"Hepatica in bloom, spring beauty and cutleaf toothworts starting to bloom, elm and red maple in bloom."
—from preserve manager's notes

Spring wildflowers are influenced heavily by the weather. Obervations from 2013 to 2021 revealed variations in blooming schedules. For example, in preparation for a public wildflower program, the preserve manager visited the Shallenberger on April 17, 2015, to make a list of the plants that were blooming along the trail, including ginger. In the next year, ginger had already started to bloom on the 22nd of March, about two weeks earlier. The preserve manager's notes record the variation in blooming times across the years.

April 7, 2014:
"Serviceberry ready to bloom on Allen Knob west side.
Hepatica in bloom on north and east side of Allen Knob.
Early bloodroot blooming on east side of Allen Knob."
—from preserve manager's notes

Wild ginger (Asarum canadense) in bloom on the northeast side of Allen Knob.

April 7, 2014:

"Serviceberry ready to bloom on Allen Knob west side.
Hepatica in bloom on north and east side of Allen Knob.
Early bloodroot blooming on east side of Allen Knob."

—from preserve manager's notes

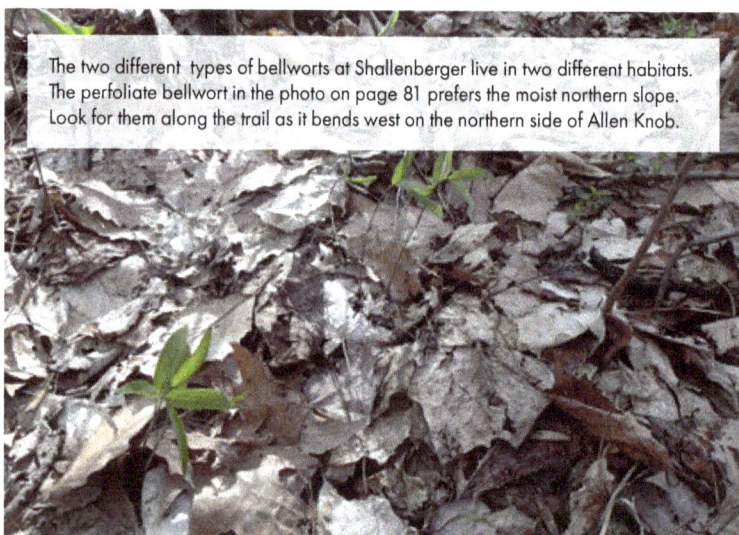

The two different types of bellworts at Shallenberger live in two different habitats. The perfoliate bellwort in the photo on page 81 prefers the moist northern slope. Look for them along the trail as it bends west on the northern side of Allen Knob.

Sessile bellwort (Uvularia sessilifolia). Find this plant early on the southern side of Allen Knob, just to the left of the staircase. In this photo, the plant is not in bloom. Bellworts are classic spring ephemerals. They bloom early and die before the trees leaf out.

Violets usually begin their wildflower parade on the southern side of Allen Knob. John Eastman writes of them in his 1992 *The Book of Forest and Thicket* "as a pilot light that ignites the entire burst of resurrection we call spring." They have colonized the younger woods due to their ant-dispersed seeds and tolerance for disturbances. Species of violet that are found at Shallenberger include the blue violets pictured on page 84 along

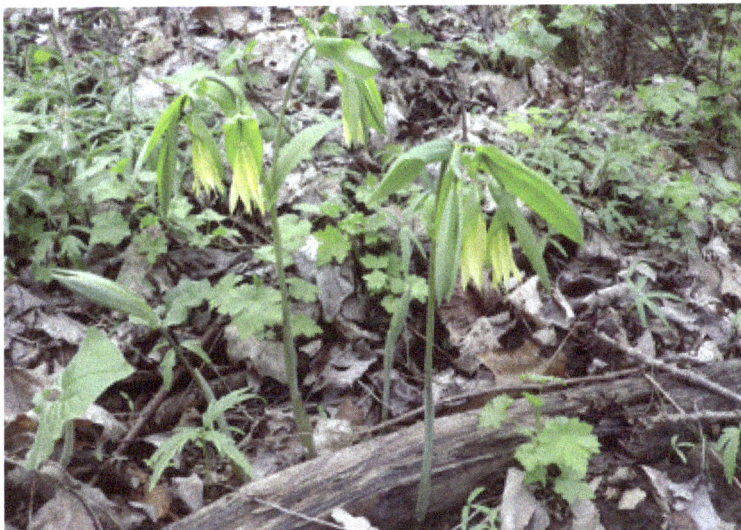

Perfoliate bellwort (uvularia perfoliata) .

Rue anemone (thalictrum thalictroides), a true spring ephemeral.
The whole plant disappears shortly after blooming.

with the smooth yellow violet (*Viola pensylvanica*) and the wood violet (*Viola palmata*).

April 11, 2015:

"smooth rockcress ready to bloom southeast corner Allen Knob. Spring beauties peak bloom, with ulvalaria emerging. Basal leaves of Alumroot along upper staircase. Up high springcress, toothworts, trillium on the north side. Serviceberry with flower buds on top of Allen Knob, early saxifrage also with flower buds. First ginger bloom, large flowered trillium and bellwort on the north side."

—from preserve manager's notes

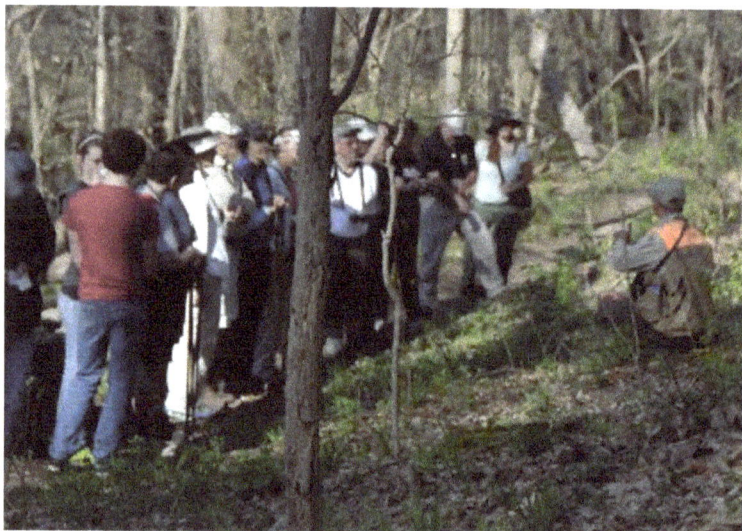

Wildflower identification program, May 16, 2015.

March 22, 2016:
"Rue anemone in bloom. Ginger starting to bloom.
Flies and bees on blooming hepatica."
—from preserve manager's notes

It can be hard to separate spring wildflower-viewing from birding. Around the middle of April, migratory birds start to arrive to supplement the singing heard in the trees from winter residents. Tufted titmice are especially noisy in the preserve as they break apart from the more social foraging flocks. Watch younger maples and hickories for the yellow-bellied sapsuckers as they make a food stop on their way north. Just past the turn to the Allen Knob spur trail, watch the ravine below and toward

Anise Root, (Osmorhiza longistylis), a second shift
bloomer. Photo courtesy of Judd Clover.

the south to see migrants and foraging flocks. Another good spot is on the extreme northern part of the trail, below Ruble Knob. Watch the treeline to the north as it borders a utility cut that runs through the preserve, as well as the ravine to the west. As spring matures, the tulip poplar-dominated forest on the western side of the Ruble Knob Trail is a good place to see Kentucky warblers.

April 18, 2012:
"Bellwort blooming below the rocks.
Jack-in-the-pulpit emerging. Scarlet Tanager by
the parking lot. Sweet cicely ready to bloom."
—from preserve manager's notes

Common blue violet (viola papilionacea). Photo courtesy of Judd Clover.

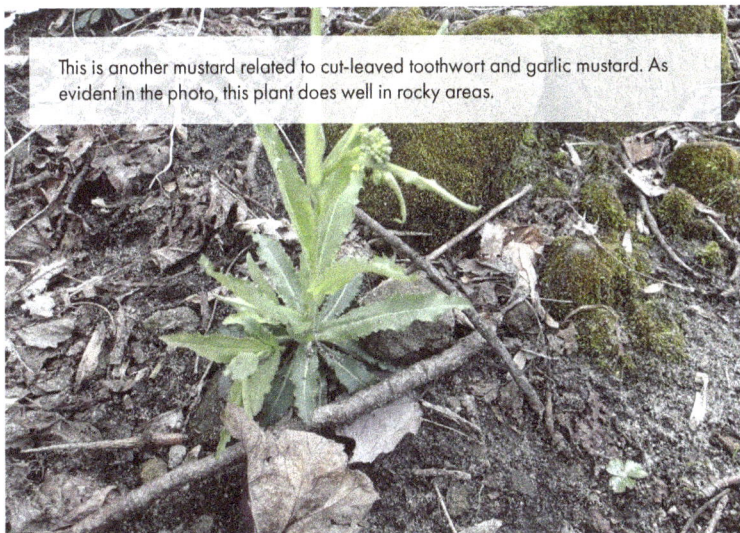

This is another mustard related to cut-leaved toothwort and garlic mustard. As evident in the photo, this plant does well in rocky areas.

Smooth rockcress (arabis laevigata) preparing to bloom.

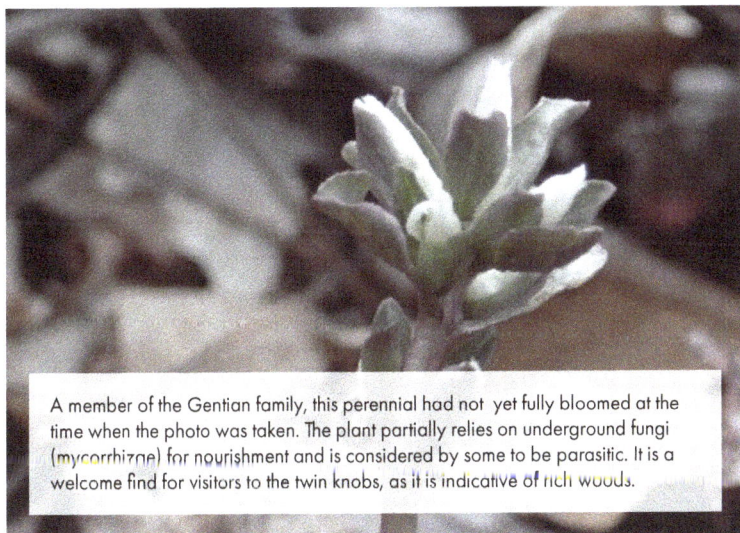

A member of the Gentian family, this perennial had not yet fully bloomed at the time when the photo was taken. The plant partially relies on underground fungi (mycorrhizae) for nourishment and is considered by some to be parasitic. It is a welcome find for visitors to the twin knobs, as it is indicative of rich woods.

The pennywort (obolaria virginica) was found on the northern side of Allen Knob on April 1, 2021.

April 26, 2012:
"Trillium grandiflorum (large flowered trillium) in full bloom north side of Allen Knob. Saxifraga virginiensis (early saxifrage) in full bloom. Ranunculus abortivus (kidney leaved buttercup) in bloom. Ribes cynosbati (gooseberry) starting to bloom. Arabis laevigata (smooth rock cress) setting siliques, south side of Allen Knob (on 28 May the siliques were still green and had not split)."

—from preserve manager's notes

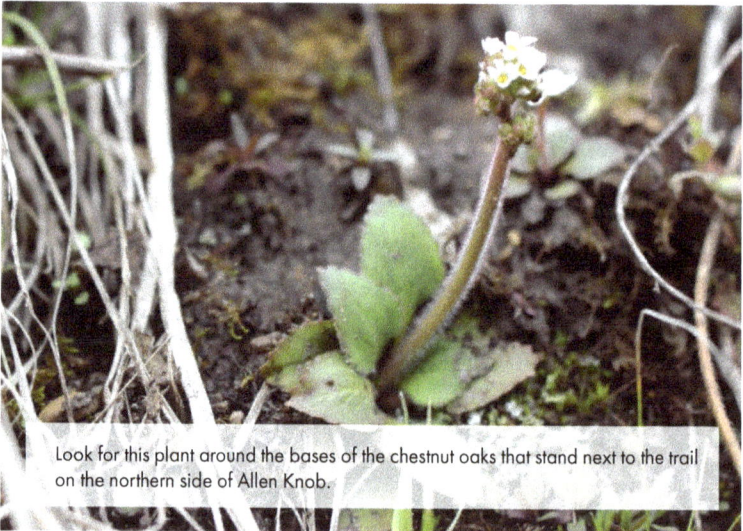

Look for this plant around the bases of the chestnut oaks that stand next to the trail on the northern side of Allen Knob.

Early saxifrage (saxifraga virginiensis).

As April closes out, another wave of wildflowers moves to the forefront with the arrival of "second shift" flowers. The trillium will hang around into May, but hepatica, uvularias, spring beauties, cut-leaved toothworts, and rue anemone begin to wither away. Wild geraniums start to bush out as their flower buds develop, jack-in-the-pulpits start to show up everywhere, and in the trillium patches, the majority of flowers turn from white to pink as they age.

Waterleaf takes over the southeastern slope of Allen Knob, showcasing their attractive mottled leaves and white fuzzy flowers. Mayapple patches, consisting of root connected clones, punctuated by the expanding leaves of summer forbs, start to dress up the bare southern slope. Everywhere, sweet cicely and anise root present their small, white flowers to eager pollinators.

May 2, 2017:

"Trillium grandiflorum (large flowered trillium) past peak north side of Allen Knob. Ozmorhiza spp. (sweet cicely and aniseroot) In bloom (peak). Geranium maculatum (wild geranium) in peak bloom. Podophyllum peltatum (mayapple) just past peak bloom. Orchis spectabalis (Showy orchis) in bloom along ruble knob trail. Aplectrum hymale (puttyroot): winter leaves gone, no sign of seed stem. Polygonatum spp (Solomon's seal) in bloom, more mature on the south slope. Smilicina racemosa (false solomon's seal) opening, racemose flowering pattering. Uvualarias (bellworts) appear done."

—from preserve manager's notes

Ruble Knob displays much of the same plant life, in addition to two members of the orchid family: showy orchis and putty root. Soon after the appearance of these plants, Solomon's seal and Solomon's plume start blooming as well. Watch the gooseberry for their interesting flowers on both north slopes along with the spicebush. Overhead, trees leaf out, and the forest floor becomes shaded. As May 1st arrives, it is easy to forget to look down as migratory birds start arriving around the knobs in earnest. The ground starts to green up, and more flowers begin to appear.

May 24, 2012:
"smartweeds emerging. Hydrangea arborescens (hydrangea) in bloom. Gooseberry with green striped fruit. Botrychium virginianum with fertile stalk (rattlesnake fern), false Solomons seal starting to bloom."

—from preserve manager's notes

Flies and bees depend on these early blooming flowers. Big, fuzzy flies (bombyliidae) emerge with the arrival of cooler temperatures. On a warm day, watch the dark bees and flies dart among the flowers, especially the spring beauties, in search of pollen and nectar. The fly, which has longer mouth parts, can also successfully reach into the tubular toothwort flowers. Once the weather rises above fifty degrees, bumblebees start to hover low over the forest floor.

Wild geraniums (geranium maculatum), with small native bees resting in the flowers. The bees may be early flying Andrenidae. This photo was taken May 6, 2013.

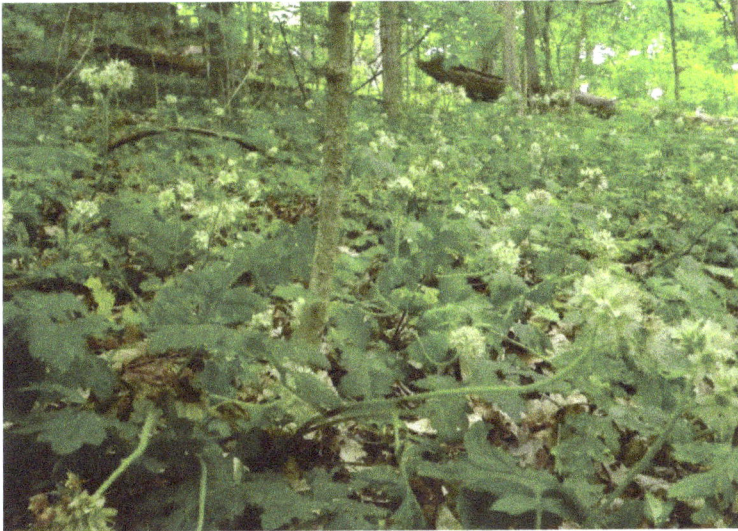

Hairy waterleaf (hydrophyllum macrophyllum) putting on a spectacular show on the southeast side of Allen Knob. This photo was taken on May 21, 2015.

False Solomon's seal or Solomon's plume (Maianthemum racemosum). May 19, 2014.

The photo on the left was taken on May 16, 2013, of putty root (Aplectrum hymale) with flowerbuds. On May 27, 2014, the preserve manager stated, "Putty root was recorded as in bloom." These orchids can be found in various places along the base of Ruble Knob. Unlike most plants, they sport leaves and conduct photosynthesis during the fall and winter, while the leaves die out in the spring before the flower stalks emerge. The photo on the right was taken on April 12, 2013. Like all orchids, these plants should not be disturbed.

Putty Root (Aplectrum hymale).

Perhaps the most delicate plants that the preserve hosts are the orchids. Orchids require specific fungal relationships in the soils and duff to thrive. As will be discussed later in this book, deer, humans, and earthworms can be hazardous to orchids.

This photo was taken on May 16, 2013. Showy Orchis (Orchis spectabilis) in bloom along the trail on the south side of Ruble Knob.

*In late May and early June, wild hydrangea (hydrangea arborescens)
adorns the rocky slopes. Climbing the staircase on Allen Knob is a
great place to get up close to this woody-stemmed plant.*

May 27, 2019:
*"honewort in bloom, bottle brush grass flowering, pond-
hawk in flight along trail on southside of Allen Knob.
Waterleaf in decline. Hydrangea with flower buds.
Mountain laurel in bloom. Maple leaf viburnum in flower
bud. Putty root in bloom on west side of Allen Knob above
the trail. Kentucky warbler still singing on the north side of
the honeysuckle trail. Large alternate leaf dogwood center
mass on the north side of Allen Knob."*
—from preserve manager's notes

The hike around the twin knobs starts by passing the dedication plaque and continuing on through a young sugar maple and

black cherry forest that hugs the downhill side of the trail almost until it reaches the three sisters tulip poplar tree. The relatively uniform size of the darker cherry and lighter maple tree trunks reveals that it is a young forest.

Most hikers who are on scheduled programs treat the less mature woods as "flyover country," or better said, "walk on by" portions of the trail. The more coveted flowers are not there. Perhaps it is controversial to say, but some flowers seem to be more treasured than others when strictly speaking about native wildflowers. Some flowers seem to be viewed as "quality wildflowers," which can be defined as the plants that bring the cameras and cell phones out for photos while the interpreter stops to identify and explain them. A second characteristic of these "quality wildflowers" is that they favor the more mature woods. It seems ironic that trees return before the native, "quality" forbs that live in their shade.

July 21, 2012:
"Silene stellata along trail on southwest side of allen knob. Ebony spleenwort on west side of allen knob. Hydrastis canadensis golden seal w plants n. side of allen knob. r/o Agrimony gryposepela in bloom, small yellow flowers. Campunula americana tall bellflower in bloom. Agertina altissima white snakeroot starting to bloom. Passiflora lutea yellow passionflower in bloom in along trail south of Allen Knob."
—from preserve manager's notes

The explanation for this lies beyond human-made values and is grounded in actual ecology. Rarity can make anything valuable, so we can start by questioning why these plants are becoming rare. Reasons for this include disturbances, deer, non-native invasive plants, and earthworms. As will be discussed in more detail in the chapter "Protecting the Remnants," deer eat too many plants, invasive plants take up space where the wildflowers would otherwise grow, and earthworms change the soil from its native state. These reasons should suffice for now.

We still have quite an array of plants that do well despite the deer, invaders, and worms. They are not quite as showy as others, usually having small white or greenish flowers. The carrot family supplies quite a few plants to the preserve as early summer arrives, in addition to sweet cicely and anise root. The sides of the trail also display black snakeroots (*Sanicula* spp.), honeworts

*Starry campion (silene stellata) on the southwest side of
Allen Knob confirms that summer is here.*

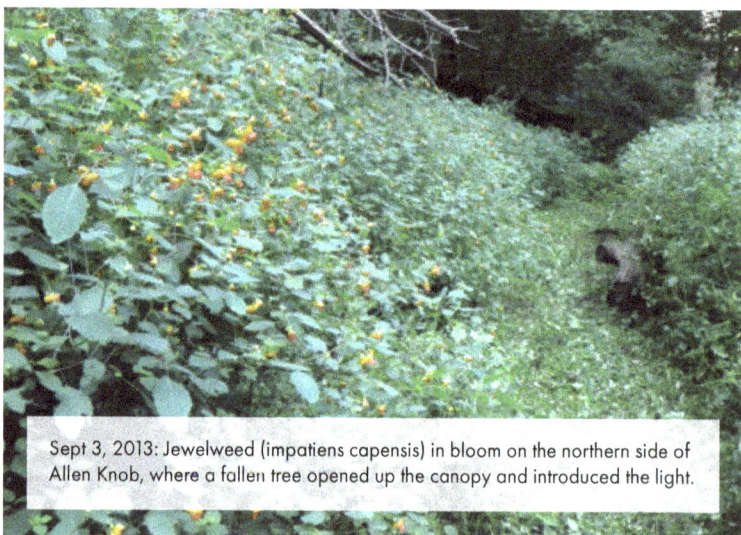

Sept 3, 2013: Jewelweed (impatiens capensis) in bloom on the northern side of Allen Knob, where a fallen tree opened up the canopy and introduced the light.

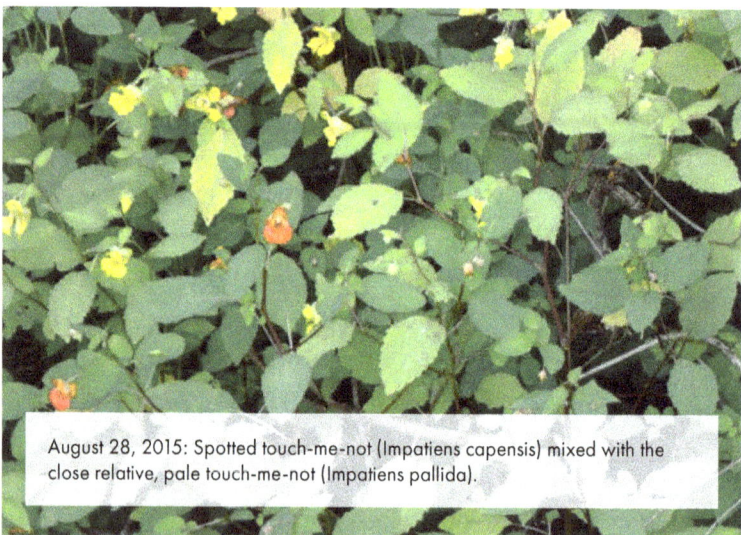

August 28, 2015: Spotted touch-me-not (Impatiens capensis) mixed with the close relative, pale touch-me-not (Impatiens pallida).

(*Cryptotaenia canadensis*), and the small, whorled-leaved galiums from the Cleaver family. As the summer progresses, these small flowers, however insignificant they may be to us, are important to the insects that pollinate or eat them. Striking flowers will also appear, however: the next two pages feature three plants that are large and dramatic enough to get visitors' attention as summer moves along.

August 28, 2017:
"Horsebalm in peak bloom n.e. Allen Knob (Collinsonia canadensis) Indian tobacco (Lobelia inflata) by the glacial erratic n.w. Allen Knob. Touch me nots (Impatiens capensis), south and north side of Allen Knob, starry campion (Silene stellata in bloom w. side of Allen Knob."
—from preserve manager's notes

As summer moves into fall, asters and goldenrods take the third and final shift of flowering. Wreath goldenrod lines the spur trail that winds around Allen Knob, while woodland asters put on a flourish by the trails in shades of blue and white.

September 21, 2012:
"wreath goldenrod Solidago caesia in bloom on Allen Knob. Along trail southeast of Allen knob: carpenter's square Scrophularia marilandica. Clearweed (Pilea pumila) throughout. White Snakeroot Eupatorium rugosum fall bloom is done."
—from preserve manager's notes

*August 28, 2015: Tall bellflower (Campanula americana)
near a stand of jewelweed on Allen Knob.*

As fall moves into winter, hepatica and trillium, already hidden in the soil, wait patiently for the spring equinox. Over the countless years that have passed since the ice fled north, this cycle has continued: the flush of spring ephemerals, the summer durables, and finally, the fall goldenrods and asters.

Fall ends in a burst of color and then it all falls to the ground. The bare limbs of the trees remain crowded together on the ridges, appearing in drab shades of brown and gray. Like funeral mourners pressed together maybe they mourn for a quieter past hidden in the deep folds of their DNA. Looking closely, little splotches of green remain in the hardy lichens and mosses. Looking closer still, life is hiding in the buds of the trees and shrubs and in the corms and buds underground.

Lichens and Birds, November 6, 2016:
"redbellied woodpecker at trail entrance. Rough speckled shield lichen (Plantalia rudecta ODNR 52) on chestnut oak on top of Allen Knob. Allen Knob at honeycomb weathering r/o Lepraria neglecta ODNR 18 zoned dust lichen.

Pair of Carolina wrens at the bridge. Nuthatches and chickadees along the honeysuckle loop.

On a fallen hickory limb. Lemon lichen Candelaria concolor and Pyscia millegran Powdery rosette lichen.

Common greenshield Flavoparmelia caperata and fluffy dust Leparia lobificans on red maple."
—from preserve manager's notes

The summer songsters are long gone, the Kentucky warbler having already passed Kentucky and kept going. A hardy bunch of flocking chickadees, tufted titmice, cardinals, towhees, golden crowned kinglets and bluejays will stay. Coming in from the north white throated sparrows will join them. A persitant hiker might even get to see a brown creeper or overwintering yellow bellied sapsucker.

The plants that participate in this yearly cycle are tough yet fragile. Reconsider the young forest by the trail entrance: cherries and maples easily reconquered the old fields, but our lifetimes may pass before hepatica and trillium can be found there again. The toughest job may be protecting the remnants.

PROTECTING THE REMNANTS

HIKERS IN THE SPRING may be startled when rounding the trail on Allen Knob or approaching Ruble knob by the sound of the unmistakable babble of humans elbowing its way through the chatter of birds. The first clue that something is happening is more cars than usual in the parking lot, along with a state vehicle or two. The second clue is a pile of packs and lunches beside the

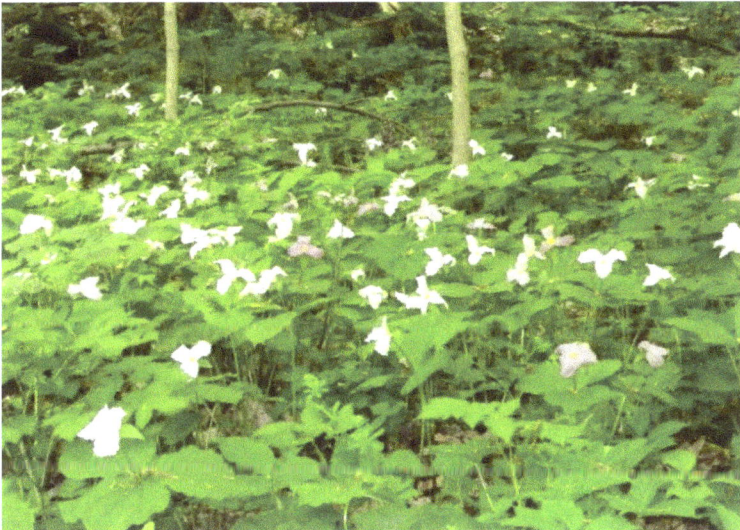

Native grand flowered trillium in peak bloom on the northern side of Allen Knob in April.

trail, and the third is a group of filled trash bags sitting on the side of the trail. The first thought may be that a litter clean-up is going on, which is partially correct. It is a cleanup, but of a different kind of litter, the kind that is green and growing: garlic mustard (*Alliaria petiolata*).

Non-native and invasive garlic mustard on the western side of Allen Knob in late April.

The majority of hikers, runners, cyclists, and disc golfers that visit our parks and preserves today do not know the difference between native and non-native plant species because we have lost our knowledge of North American natural history. Not all extirpations or extinctions can be attributed *directly* to man; however, with the arrival of Columbus on the continent in 1492, the Columbian Exchange began. After that, European settlements and the development of global trade spread European and Asian species across the oceans, reshaping the plant and animal communities in North America.

Plant, fungi, and animal species traveled back and forth between the continents, starting an ecological war between natives and non-natives that only intensified with time. Invasions by non-native plant species are now the number two cause of plant extinctions across the world, second only to habitat loss. That loss of plants to extinction or extirpation elicits concern for the animals that depend on them.

If past glacial and quarrying impacts were not bad enough for the twin knobs, they then had to endure the uncomfortable encroachment of unfamiliar plants and animals that impacted them like a bad skin rash. The exchange of native and non-native

After pulling, the garlic mustard is bagged up and
"cooked" for a season to kill the seeds before dumping out.

species hit Fairfield County and the knobs very quickly, and it almost seemed like native plants were replaced by non-native plants overnight. This quote, taken from A. A. Graham's *History of Fairfield and Perry Counties* was written only 132 years after Christopher Gist and his party first explored the area in which the preserve is found today and only 80 years after Ohio became a state:

> *There were likewise in the wild and new condition of the country almost innumerable varieties of stinking weeds, grasses and plants that are scarcely to be seen at all now, while hundreds of varieties not found here at first have taken their place.*[21]

Succession[22] along the edge is a tricky business now and has morphed into a hybrid blending of old and new worlds, resulting in surprising emergent behaviors between the species, both native and immigrant.

Multiflora rose, a thorny invasive plant, must have arrived on the knobs many years ago (maybe before 1900) and taken full advantage of the open grounds. Once agriculture was abandoned, the plant figuratively stormed the ramparts, robbing the slopes of normal succession and causing the trees to force themselves through the rose to grow. Some species were successful, but others were not. Under the rosa, the forest forbs lost their place.

---

21 Graham, A. A., 1883. *History of Fairfield and Perry Counties Ohio.* Chicago, W.H. Beers & Company. Accessed at http://www.perrycountyohio.us/fphhistory/fphpart3/.

22 Succession is the changing of plant and animal species over the years from an open field to a mature forest. It works differently in prairie and desert areas. Kricher and Morrison's 1998 *Eastern Forests* defines succession. Their work fails to account for the invasive non-native plant species that now usurp traditional succession in central Ohio.

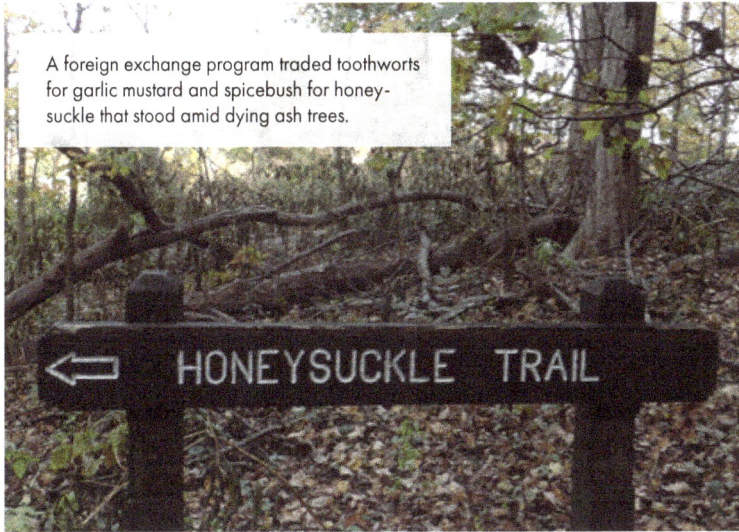

A foreign exchange program traded toothworts for garlic mustard and spicebush for honeysuckle that stood amid dying ash trees.

HONEYSUCKLE TRAIL

The trail below Ruble Knob on the eastern side of the preserve.

The trail on the eastern side of the preserve below Ruble Knob originally was named the Honeysuckle Trail, referring to *Lonicera japonica,* or Japanese honeysuckle. This evergreen vine with bird-dispersed fruits climbed over the edge of the trail and covered what it could, almost like a miniature version of the kudzu vine that was covering southern states. Nobody seemed to notice or care that the native habitats didn't look like the pictures in the field guides.

DNAP personnel and volunteers have worked to control and lessen the influence that the multiflora has exerted over its plant neighbors. They have help now in the form of a disease that is also affecting domesticated roses: rose rosette virus. As forest trees recover, Japanese honeysuckle seems to wither away in the shade, becoming nothing more than a tangling of vines along the edges of the path.

Passenger pigeons depended heavily on beech trees. At one time, the pigeons' flights "resembled the windings of a vast and majestic river," but market hunting and logging put an end to it. The last passenger pigeon died in the Cincinnati Zoo in 1914. The twins probably felt a sense of emptiness when the flights finally ceased and the sky grew quiet.

Looking over Allen Knob near two beech trees.

By the turn of the century, the ecology of the area had changed drastically with many species lost forever: the passenger pigeon and the Carolina parakeet were either gone or on their way to extinction. The large predators and mammals, such as pumas, wolves, elk, and woodland bison were no longer wild in the state. Even the whitetail deer had plunged almost to extirpation[23] before staging a tremendous recovery in the last few decades.

Native diseases, predators, parasites, or browsers may not necessarily follow a plant or animal to a new continent. In that case, the immigrant can grow and spread unimpeded, a condition termed ecological release. In the case of the multiflora rose, a disease eventually caught up to it: small, twisted, reddish clusters of

---

23 Extinction is the permanent loss of a species from the globe. Extirpation is the loss of a species from an area, such as a state or country.

excessively thorny growths found on the ends of the vines could mean that the rosa is running out of time.

Garlic mustard on the left, native cut leaf toothwort on the right.

The quality native wildflowers on the northern side of the Allen and Ruble Knobs contend with another insidious invader who has not yet faced any enemies on this continent: the greenery in the photo on the left is almost a pure mono-culture of the invasive garlic mustard. By contrast, cut-leaved toothwort, in the photo on the right, lights up the slopes of Shallenberger every spring. Ironically, as happens with many invasive species, both plants are in the same family and share the same habitat requirements. Once garlic mustard monopolizes an area, the toothwort is one of the first plants to disappear.

Garlic mustard may be one of the most-studied invaders in the country. Armed with "novel weapons," the plant quickly subdued the mesic-rich soils[24] of forests in the eastern United States. A native of Europe and Asia, it is believed[25] that garlic mustard was brought to Long Island by immigrants in 1868 and escaped soon after. The plant has been a subject of controversy, causing interested parties to join one of two sides: the "pull crowd" or the "don't pull crowd."

As happens in all preserves in Ohio, professional staff developed a Preserve Management Plan to guide the preserve manager. Garlic mustard and multiflora rose are both labeled as a "frequent" occurrence at the preserve. In 2017, the preserve manager summarized some the garlic mustard study plots on the northern slope of Allen Knob: *"Each of the current plots contains 3.14 square meters (one meter circle around a point). The west area contains 35 plots with a measured area of 110.95 square meters. November of 2016 revealed 250 plants in the plots with a mean of 2.27 plants per square meter. The east plot contains 30 plots with a measured area of 94.2 square meters with 1.01 plants per square meter. We will be starting our fifth year of treating garlic mustard in this area and we do see significant declines that I hope are not the result of a biennial cycle."* Each year, the staff and volunteers attack this plant in the triaged[26] areas. Each year, there is the hope that the population is decreasing.

The staff has been very successful at controlling the the tree of heaven (*Ailanthus altissima*), despite the presence of a seed

---

24 Soils are categorized into three types based on their moisture levels: hydric (wetlands), mesic (moist, like the northern side of Allen Knob), and xeric (dry, like the shallow soils on ridges).

25 For more information on invasive plants checkout the Invasive Plant List of Ohio Invasive Plants from the Ohio Department of Agriculture.

26 Annually, the preserve manager develops an ecomanagement plan (EMP) to supplement the Preserve Management Plan. The EMP chooses what to do, as well as where, when, and how to control invasive species during that year. Areas are triaged, or given priority, based on several factors, including the quality native species present.

source near the preserve's western boundary. Staff and volunteers have also controlled the vine winter creeper (*Euonymus fortunei*) and its shrubby cousin, winged wahoo (*Euonymus alatus*).

Spilling over from the till plains to the west, bush honeysuckle is a scary invader that requires constant vigilance already dominating areas. Travelers driving from Columbus to Lancaster may not know it completely covers the fencerows along the highway. Refer back to the photo in Chapter Four: bush honeysuckle leafs out earlier and works later into the fall, which provides it with a growth advantage over native shrub layer species.

More recently, chickweed, *Stellaria media*, is becoming a species of concern for some land managers, though it is not necessarily listed as invasive on official documentation yet.

Chickweed on the northeastern side of Allen Knob. Originally an immigrant garden weed, this plant spread very fast in the rich mesic soils found in forests. The dense green mats rob younger plants of nutrients and space. November 7, 2023.

Off-trail movement, whether it be climbing on rocks or morel hunting, damages sensitive native plants and creates soil disturbance.

Eurasian species, such as chickweed and garlic mustard, had been following the domesticated animals and steel plows of Eurasia long before their introduction to North America. They became dependent on soil surface disturbance to gain a foothold in their growth. These plants have short lives and high seed distribution, but loss of canopy due to windthrows or tree deaths gives these invaders access to sunlight and other resources that allow them to conquer an area. By contrast, our high-value wildflowers have long lives and, in many cases, depend on ants to spread their seeds.

Non-native plant species do not leave the twins in a botanical vacuum. Like any war, there is collateral damage: the loss of native shrubs threatens birds and insects alike. Ironically, it is animals, including humans, that spread these non-native plants. Garlic mustard and Japanese stiltgrass seeds are picked up by fur, footpads, or footwear and moved out away from the source.

Bush honeysuckle is a nutrition-poor substitute for native fruits such as dogwood and spicebush, yet native and non-native birds eat them readily. After passing through the digestive system, the hard seed is defecated out. Two members of the euonymus family, the winter creeper and the burning bush, are both spread by ingestion and defecation and are found within the preserve.

Threats to the preserve extend beyond invasive plants. Under the heading "Potential Ecological Threats," the Preserve Management Plan includes impacts from whitetail deer, non-native earthworms, and the emerald ash borer. With the loss of

Deer browsing on the eastern side of Allen Knob on October 17, 2017. This photo was taken from the trail. Notice the deer's partially raised tail, which reveals that while the deer is somewhat disturbed by the hiker, he is not afraid enough to leave the area.

native predators, despite the prevalence of hunting, deer populations have risen to troubling densities as they overbrowse native plants and find their way into the middle of our roads. Ironically, if deer would graze non-native and invasive species, rather than native species, there wouldn't be a problem.

Overgrazing is a problem resulting in negative feedback to native plants. Without year-round predators, deer can graze in one spot without feeling unsafe. As a result, deer heavily browse native plants, leaving holes in the habitat that are readily occupied by non-native plants such as garlic mustard. As garlic mustard populations expand, deer and other wildlife move through infected areas and inadvertently transport seeds to new areas.

15 September 2015:
*"The grapes were plentiful up in the top and showed up in
the binoculars. It was nice, while the parking lot was still
mostly empty to watch the two yellow rump warblers forage
through the grapes. With a sudden whir of wings a flock of
starlings came out of nowhere and covered the grape vines.
Within minutes the starlings and the grapes were gone."*
—from preserve manager's notes

Earthworms are another problem that is not well known
outside of ecology circles. The ice that once pounded against
Allen and Ruble also left glaciated Ohio without earthworms.
However, the movement of European plants along with the settlers brought non-native worms right up to the knobs. Quite
surprisingly, worms are good for gardens and fields, but not
for forests. Earthworms eat practically the entire duff layer,
which in turn changes the soil composition. Decomposers such
as fungi, bacteria, and arthropods disappear. Amphibians that
depend on the duff layer for food and shelter disappear. Native
plants that depend on fungi for symbiotic relationships disappear. Not all of this is bad news, however: just as Allen and
Ruble withstood the glaciers with their sandstone armor, the
acidity of their iron oxide-cemented rocks discourage worm
invasion on the knobs. The proof is in the presence of trillium,
bloodroot, and various orchids that tend to disappear as a result
of earthworm invasions.

Long associations with human habitations from Eurasia
enabled the imported starling and English sparrow to threaten
and displace native birds. Movement of North American species

eastward includes the nest parasites, cowbirds, further stressing native songbirds who are nesting within Shallenberger.

Protecting the preserve from the most invasive species of all, *Homo sapiens*, requires a safe and accessible trail system, as well as clear rules. At Shallenberger, the rules are posted on a bulletin board at the entrance, along with seasonal information and a preserve map. On the left is a boot brush under a kiosk explaining the impact of invasive plant species. The other signs inform visitors that pets and bikes are not permitted on the trail and instruct them not to gather or disturb any of the natural materials in the preserve.

The boot brush is both symbolic and practical: hikers arriving at Shallenberger may bring seeds trapped on the soles or lugs of their footwear. Pets are not allowed for a couple of reasons. For example, pets urinating or defecating may introduce disease to

This plant requires a mature, stable forest environment to thrive. This photo was taken on May 13, 2014, on the northern side of Ruble Knob, courtesy Judd Clover.

Spotted wintergreen (Chimaphila umbellata).

the resident wildlife. Pets may also chase wildlife or range off the trails. Off-trail movement disturbs the soil and moves non-native seeds. Gathering wildflowers, mushrooms, or any other natural object is not permitted on state nature preserves. The obvious reason for this rule is inherent in the title: preserve.

DNAP volunteer Judd Clover repairing a bridge damaged after a tree fell. This photo was taken in August of 2013.

Natural history includes all the native living things, even those that are under siege, in either forgotten or protected enclaves that creative destruction somehow missed. Trying to decide which species is native and which is not is controversial.

Perhaps the simplest place to start is just prior to statehood; that would be before the first honeysuckle or garlic mustard showed up on the knobs.

For some of us, preservation means holding onto our self-identity in a world gone mad with development. How can the progress of a glaciated tundra that self-developed into a beautiful, temperate forest not be termed development equal to any manmade project. Natural history must reach beyond academic discussion, or extinctions will continue to dry up the pool of animals and plants available for contribution to ecological systems.

Some folks will argue that preservation should be limited to sites that contain specific endangered plants, animals, or geologic features. In central Ohio, especially along the glaciated edge, very little wild land not completely inundated with Eurasian influence exists. It is not the intention of this discussion to list all the problems that natural systems face but simply to say that any spot that still harbors small surviving slices of native ecosystems should be salvaged. The story of this small preserve should encourage us to be more aware, or, dare say, woke.

Preservation begins with supporting the natural area programs in your area. Perhaps the most extreme threat to preserves across the state is possible future loss of funding for natural area programs. For the twins at Shallenberger, it is the Department of Natural Areas and Preserves under the Ohio Department of Natural Resources. Show your support; check out their website and consider the tax checkoff.

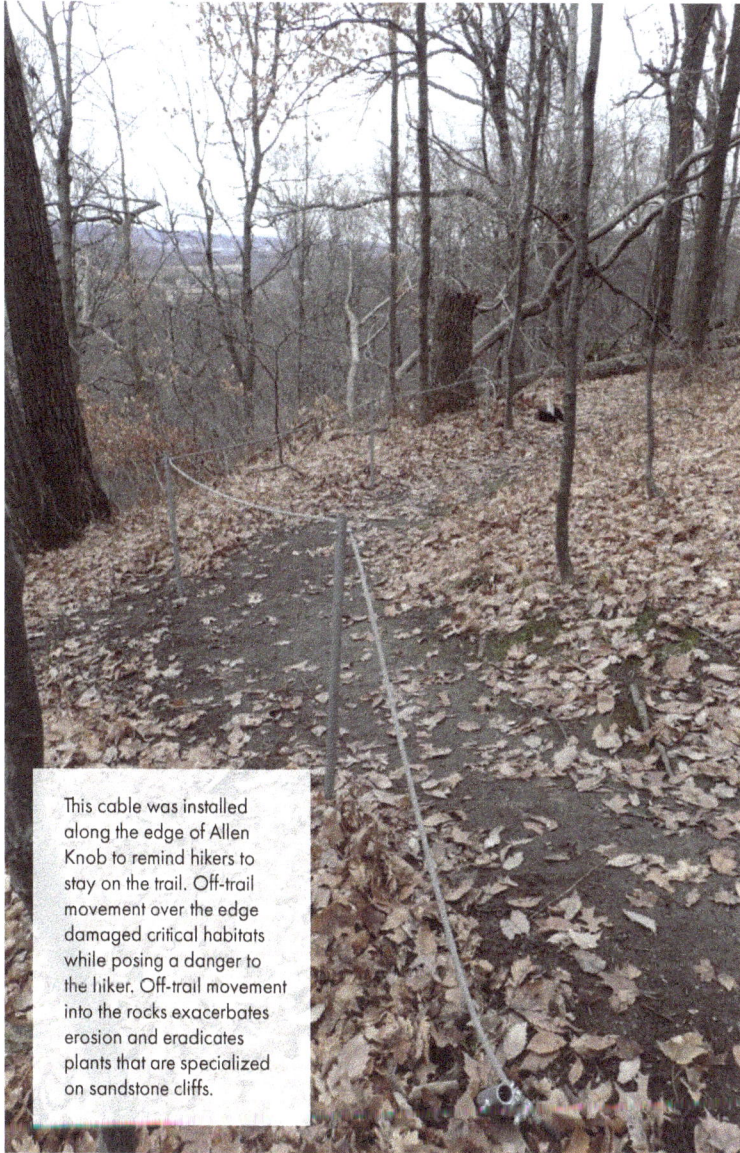

This cable was installed along the edge of Allen Knob to remind hikers to stay on the trail. Off-trail movement over the edge damaged critical habitats while posing a danger to the hiker. Off-trail movement into the rocks exacerbates erosion and eradicates plants that are specialized on sandstone cliffs.

Cable Railing at Allen Knob.

Blooming mountain laurel. May 16, 2013, Rhode Cove State Nature Preserve.

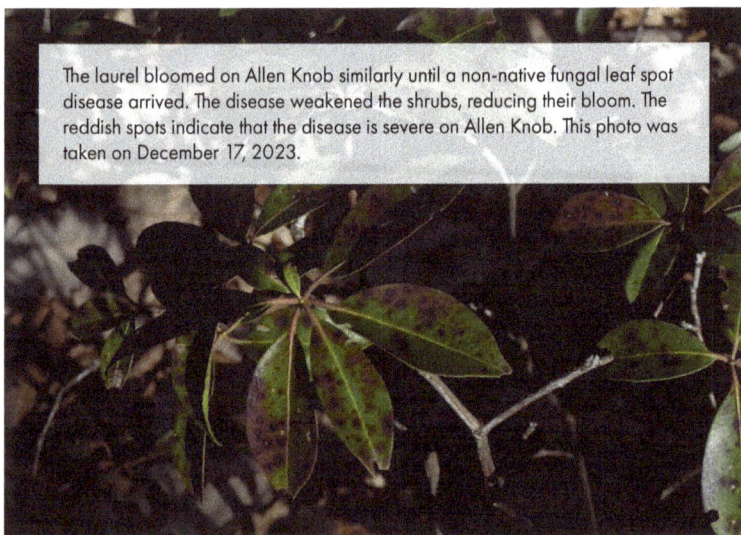

The laurel bloomed on Allen Knob similarly until a non-native fungal leaf spot disease arrived. The disease weakened the shrubs, reducing their bloom. The reddish spots indicate that the disease is severe on Allen Knob. This photo was taken on December 17, 2023.

Mountain laurel on Allen Knob

Staircase built November of 2023 replacing the older stairs up to the top of Allen Knob.

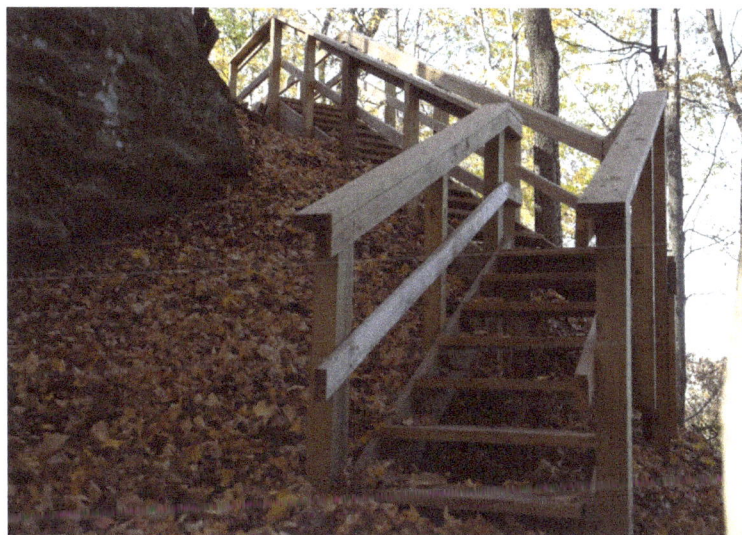

Using the stairs protects the fragile soils and plants on the steep slopes.

ALLEN AND RUBLE

BORN FROM THE CRUMBS of ancient mountains, hardened by the sea, pushed up into the light, riding an arch up and out of the waves came two siblings, Allen and Ruble.

Fresh and youthful they stood on the edge of a great plateau, guarding the dark hills behind them

Creeping on ponderous feet, the sea came back as ice.

Great, surging tides of cold hard glacier ground granite mercenaries against the sandstone armor.

Brother and sister did not yield, the ice fled, and time marched on.

Allen and Ruble felt the gentle tickle as peoples plodded after great hairy beasts on soft soled moccasins

Mountain laurel garnished their rocky edges, mighty oaks and chestnuts dressed the ridges, and ash and elm decked the slopes.

While tanagers sang happy songs from leafy perches, hepatica and trillium dotted the dark soil with earthbound stars

The plains before them bowed in honor and time quietly marched on.

To the east, beyond the green hills, dark clouds gathered as white sailed ships brought a storm.

The peoples, in their soft-soled moccasins were swept away in a rabid, angry tide while hob-nailed boots punched the two siblings like a hurricane.

A Scotsman read from the Bible as hammer drills and gunpowder splintered the sandstone crowns into shreds of rubble

He built a cemetery of stone, ripped from the siblings' sides, for presidents that would never lie there.

After the thunder, the trees came creeping back, the mighty chestnut lost forever.

An act of love bought the twins a respite and a chance to heal.

A foreign exchange program traded toothworts for garlic mustard and spicebush for honeysuckle, standing amid dying ash trees.

The tanager has to sing louder now, for the quiet is gone; the storm still eddies around them while the Scotsman lies quietly in his cemetery of stone that he stole from the brother and sister.

Though ageless, the two siblings are tattered and worn, having endured the tides of ice and men.

And time marches on…

ABOUT THE AUTHOR

AFTER RETIREMENT from career life, I was finally able to do something that I really enjoyed. Working as a volunteer, conservation worker, and preserve manager for the Ohio Department of Natural Resources Division of Natural Areas and Preserves was a dream come true for too few years. Injuries and aches from previous pursuits caught up with me, and I decided to get out of the way.

My wife Roxanne, pictured in the photo on the previous page, right up there next to me on Allen Knob on a cold day (January 19, 2014), is first in line of the people I would like to thank for bearing patiently with me over the years. Next in the line is Jeff Johnson, the current director of DNAP who hired me and put up with my over-eagerness. I am also grateful to Rick Gardner, the state botanist, who had to correct my plant ID far too many times and Levi Miller, the current southeast regional manager who had to put up with me from a shared office at Boch Hollow State Nature Preserve. I would like to mention "Detroit" Duchon for constantly challenging me to think outside the box.

I had the opportunity to work with a fantastic group of volunteers: Judd Clover, Marcelle Bowen, and Esta Oneil. Along with a great group of conservation workers and other volunteers, these folks climbed hills, pushed through poison ivy, stinging nettle, and multiflora rosa, and got down on their hands and knees in all sorts of weather to save the remnants of natural history that are still left.

—Jim Osborn

BIBLIOGRAPHY

Anderson, Michael. "Is Garlic Mustard an Invader or Opportunist?" *American Scientist* 111, no. 1 (2023): 34 -41.

Braun, Lucy. *The Woody Plants of Ohio*. Columbus: Ohio State University Press, 1989.

Clemants, Steven and Gracie, Carol. 2006. *Wildflowers in the Field and Forest: A Field Guide to the Northeastern United States*. New York, Oxford University Press.

Dyer, James. 2001. "Using witness trees to assess forest change in Southeastern Ohio". *Canadian Journal of Forest Research* Vol. 31 pp 1701-1718.

Eastman, John. 1992. *The Book of Forest and Thicket*. Mechanicsburg, Stackpole Books.

Flannery, Tim. 2001. *The Eternal Frontier*. New York: Atlantic Monthly

Fores, Dan. 2022. *Wild New World*. New York: W.W. Norton

Forsyth, Jane. 1970. "A Geologist Looks at the Natural Vegetation Map of Ohio." *The Ohio Journal of Science* 70(3): 180 May, 1970.

Gracie, Carol. 2012. *Spring Wildflowers of the Northeast*. Princeton, Princeton University Press.

Gordon, Robert. 1969. The Natural Vegetation of Ohio in Pioneer Days. Columbus, The Ohio StateUniversity.

Graham, A. A., 1883. *History of Fairfield and Perry Counties Ohio*. Chicago, W.H. Beers & Company. Accessed at http://www.perrycountyohio.us/fphhistory/fphpart3/.

Hamilton, S., Deaton, M., Steigher, J., Griffin, R., Gilmore, G., Dotson, D. & Brandt, E. 2005. *Soil Survey of Fairfield County.* US Department of Agriculture and Natural Resources Conservation Service. Retrieved March 2, 2011, from soildatamart.nrcs.usda.gov/ Manuscripts/OH045/0/Fairfield_OH.pdf

Haskell, David,2012. *The Forest Unseen: A Year's Watch in Nature*. New York, Penguin Group.

Hale, Cindy. 2013. Earthworms of the Great Lakes. Kollath+Stensass, Duluth.

Hamilton,S., Deaton, M., Steiggher, J., et al. (2005) *Soil Survey of Fairfield County.* US Department of Agriculture and Natural Resources Conservation Service. Retrieved March 2, 2011, from soildatamaart.nrcs.usda.gov/Manuscripts/OH045/0/Fairfield_OH.pdf.

Hurt, Douglas R. 1996. *The Ohio Frontier: Crucible of the Old Northwest 1720-1830.* Bloomington & Indianapolis, Indiana University Press.

Knepper, G. 2002. The Official Ohio Lands Book. Ohio Auditor of State; retrieved from ohioauditor.gov/publications/docs/OhioLandsBook.pdf

Kricher, John and Morrison, Gordon, 1998. *Eastern Forests.* New York: Houghton Mifflin.

Lafferty, Michael B., ed. *Ohio's Natural History.* Columbus: The Ohio Academy of Sciences , 2003.

Matchen, D.L. & Kammer, 2006. "Incised valley fill interpretation for Mississippian Black Hand Sandstone, Appalachian Basin, USA: implications for glacial eustasy at Kinderhookian-Osagean (Tn2-Tn3) boundary". *Sedimentary Geology* 191: 89-113.

Newcomb, Lawrence. 1977. *Wildflower Guide.* New York, Little, Brown and Company.

Ohio Division of Geological Survey, 2004. Shaded drift-thickness map of Ohio. Ohio Department of Natural Resources, Division of Geological Survey Map

SG-3, generalized page-size version with text, 3 p,. scale 1:200,000.

Ohio Division of Geological Survey, 2006. Glacial Map of Ohio. Ohio Department of Natural Resources, Division of Geological Survey Map, page size with text 2p,. scale 1:200,000.

Ohio Division of Geological Survey, 2006. Bedrock Geology Map of Ohio: Ohio Department of Natural Resources, Division of Geological Survey Map BG-1, generalized page-size with text 2p,. scale 1:200,000.

Ohio Division of Geological Survey, 1998, Physiographic Regions of Ohio: Ohio Department of Natural Resources, Division of Geological Survey, page size map with text, 2 p., scale 1:2,100,000.

Invasive Plant List. Ohio Invasive Plants Council. Accessed on 1 October 2023 at https://www.oipc.info.

Invasive Plants. Ohio Department of Agriculture Invasive and Noxious Plants. accessed on 2 October, 2023 at https://agri.ohio.gov/ divisions/ plant-health/invasive-pests/ invasive-and-noxious-plants.

Roberts, David C. 1996. *Geology Eastern North America*. Boston New York: Houghton Mifflin.

Roody, William. 2003. Mushrooms of West Virginia and Central Appalachians. Lexington, University Press of Kentucky

Rule 901:5-30-01 Invasive Plant Species. 2023. Ohio Administrative Code.

Philip, Leila, 2022. *Beaver Land: How on Weird Rodent Made America*. New York, Hachette Book Group.

Scofield, Jonathan. 1800. "Township North 14, Range North 19". Ohio Historical Society.

Scott, Hervey. 1877. *A complete History of Fairfield County Ohio 1795 -1976*. Columbus, Seibert and Lilly Printers and Binders.

Solis, Michael P. "Geology of Shallenberger State Nature Preserve." *OhioGeology.com 2018*.

Van Steeg, K. 1947. "Black Hand Sandstone and conglomerate in Ohio". *Bulletin of the Geological Society of America* 58:703-727.

Wallace, David Rains. 1980. *Idle Weeds*. San Francisco: Sierra Club Books.

Wessels, Tom. 2010. *Forest Forensics*. New York, The Countryman Press.

Wolfe, Edward W.; Forsyth,
Jane L.; and Dove, George D.
Geology of Fairfield County.
Columbus: Ohio Department
of Natural Resources, Division
of Geological Survey, Bulletin
60, 1962.

www.ingramcontent.com/pod-product-compliance
Lightning Source LLC
Chambersburg PA
CBHW050844270326
41930CB00020B/3465